A GUY'S GUIDE TO LIFE

HOW TO BECOME A MAN
IN 208 PAGES OR LESS

Jason Boyett

A GUY'S GUIDE TO LIFE

© 2004 Jason Boyett

Published by W Publishing Group, a Division of Thomas Nelson, Inc., P.O. Box 141000, Nashville, Tennessee, 37214.

Transit Brand Manager: Kate Etue
Editorial Staff: Deborah Wiseman, Sunny Vann
Cover Design: Matt Lehman at Anderson Thomas Design, Nashville, Tennessee
Page Design: Lindsay Carreker

Library of Congress Cataloging-in-Publication Data

Printed in the United States of America
05 06 07 08 RRD 5 4

CONTENTS

To my parents, Mike and JoDeane Boyett.
You know you've grown up when your mom and dad
become your friends.

Acknowledgements

You can't write anything that calls itself a "guide to life" without it reflecting the wisdom of those who helped steer you along the way. So major thanks to my mom and dad, Mike & JoDeane Boyett; my in-laws, Dick & Beverly Storseth; and my grandparents, John & Mary Boyett and John & Cleta Brown. Each contributed to this book in more ways than I could count.

Special thanks to my crack team of advisers, parents, and youth experts, whose answers to a bunch of tough questions about teenage guys were instrumental in keeping the rest of these pages relevant: Darrell & Denise Anderson, Father Robert A. Busch, Jason & Leanna Craft, Jeff & Debbie Jackson, Calvin & Kristy Martin, Victor & Theresa Miller, Tommy & Lana Spencer, and Steve Trafton.

I'm also grateful to Kate Etue and the team at W Publishing for the opportunity, and to my friend Katie Meier for setting such a high standard with *A Girl's Guide to Life* (which I will admit to having read and enjoyed).

And, as always, to Aimee, Ellie, & Owen, my three favorite people in the world.

Introduction

It's right there on the cover, so it must be true: This book tells you *How to Become a Man in 208 Pages or Less*. Yes, friends, the road to manhood is an easy one. It's all picnics and butterflies and sunny days. It's like slicing cake with a chain saw. It's something you can achieve simply by reading a slim paperback for teenage guys.

Right?

Riiiiiiight. To tell the truth, that clever little subtitle—which I think is genius, by the way, if I do say so myself—is just a bit of shameless marketing. It's right up there with *Get Rock-Hard Abs in Only 7 Minutes a Day!* or all the "enlarge your manhood" spam that fills my in-box on a daily basis. Which is to say, it's a lot of hype. It's something to get your attention so you'll crack open the book and see what this "208 pages" thing is all about.

Guess what? It worked.

Unfortunately, you can't become a man in just 208 pages. Or 2,008 pages. Or by reading a book in the first place, regardless of its length. Becoming a man isn't an overnight thing. It's not something that just happens. Instead, it's a process of growing, maturing, and making good decisions—a process that starts when you're a teenager. And being a teenager? Not so easy. But you knew that already.

With that in mind, let me roll out the red carpet. Welcome, guys. Welcome to the most confusing, awkward, and exciting years of your life.

Welcome to the bad stuff. Welcome to the days when it seems everyone has it together but you. Welcome to the days when life makes absolutely no sense, when your friends and parents and siblings all seem hopelessly out of touch. Welcome to the days when you feel like the body you woke up in belongs to someone else. Welcome to the part of life we all look back on and wonder, *What the heck was I thinking?!*

On the other hand, welcome to the good stuff. Welcome to the series of changes and events and discoveries that will stick with you forever—the things you'll still remember when you're thirty or forty or sixty years old. Welcome to the years that help define who you are and who you'll be. Welcome to all the milestones that mark a guy's life. First girlfriend. First kiss. First car. Welcome to the part of life you're bound to remember with a smile, the time when you truly felt *alive.* These are the good times.

Bad stuff, good stuff. Bad times, good times. Sound interesting?

For most guys, there is no more challenging time in life than your teenage years, especially in the area between your ears. You're gonna be faced with a lot of new ideas, relationships, and situations requiring you to make the right choices. You'll start to think about things differently. You'll begin to see people differently, too—from your parents and siblings to, of course, girls. Mentally, are you up to the task?

And what about your body? If anything's true about the transition from twelve-year-old pipsqueak to eighteen-year-old man, it's that your bod will undergo a major overhaul. Changes out the wazoo. Some of them are actually pretty cool. Some of them can be really confusing. And others are, well, let's just say they're embarrassing. Lots of teen guys go through this round of physical weirdness with no clue as to what's happening. Not you, though. This book will be your tour guide through the process of growing up physically. We've got everything covered—grooming, fashion, exercise, and, yep, sex.

But becoming a man isn't all about mind and body. There's another vitally important aspect of life: your soul. Your spiritual side. It's what makes you who you are. It's what fuels your body and mind. And on the soul side of things? Big changes there, too. You'll start to ask a lot of questions—questions about the world around you, about relationships, about God. A whip-smart mind is great. So is a strong adult body. But both of those are nothing without the strength, guidance, and balance provided by your soul.

So there you have it. Mind, body, and soul. Conveniently, we've structured this entire book around those three majors. Don't feel you have to sit down and read this thing cover to cover, though. Feel free to browse. Pick a topic that looks interesting and jump right to it. Each one is packed with info. You'll find real answers to your questions (even the hard ones). You'll find tips and tricks to surviving teen life. You'll find loads of advice on how to deal with the big stuff and the small stuff. And hopefully you'll find that it's good reading, too.

Anyway, a couple of hundred pages to go before you're a man. Better get moving.

PART ONE

MIND

CHAPTER 1

MANLY MYTHS

This is probably the worst idea ever, but the first thing I want you to do as we kick-start the first chapter of the book is to (drum roll . . .) turn off your brain. Flip the mental switch. I'm going to ask you a series of multiple-choice questions, and I want you to answer them as automatically as possible. Don't think too much. In fact, don't think at all. Go with whatever pops into your head first. Ready?

1. Which of the following occupations is the most manly?
   a. Accountant
   b. Construction worker
   c. Nurse
   d. Teacher

2. If all were equally attractive, which of the guys below would the hot girls be most interested in at school?
   a. The varsity quarterback
   b. The valedictorian
   c. The first-chair violinist
   d. The yearbook editor

3. You just fell down a full flight of stairs between periods. Your backpack spilled across the floor, you're pretty sure your

ankle's broken, and something like five hundred people are now eyeing you like a monkey just climbed out of your butt. What's the proper response?

a. Ask someone to call 911.

b. Ask someone to call your mommy.

c. Ask someone for a tissue, then start crying like a baby.

d. Get up and act like you completely meant to fall down the stairs. That bone shard sticking out of your sock? Just a little scratch. Walk it off.

Ten bucks says this is how you answered, in order: Construction worker, Quarterback, and the No-big-deal approach to falling down the stairs. How do I know? Because those were my answers, too. I'm a guy, and I can guess how most guys think, even with turned-off brains. Which reminds me— time to reboot. Unknot the noodle. That's all the nonthinkage you get for the remainder of this book. Let's get started.

WHAT IS A MAN?

Most of us have a pretty good idea of what it means to be a guy. A guy is active, strong, and masculine. A guy is athletic and competitive and a natural leader. A guy is tough, macho, and doesn't show pain. He's not controlled by emotion. He's laid-back, cool, and confident in all situations. He never cries, never shows weakness. He's in charge. He's a stud.

Also: we're wrong.

We've been brainwashed by the myths of manhood. We've been snookered by male stereotypes. What's a stereotype? A stereotype is a set of beliefs about the "typical" characteristics that are supposed to apply to all members of a certain group of people—women, men, blacks, whites, Hispanics, whomever. Stereotypes can be positive or negative, and are a way for society to distinguish one group from another. Occasionally they're accurate. But mostly they're oversimplified, offensive exaggerations.

> **BIG TIP:**
> Occasionally stereotypes can be accurate, but usually they're oversimplified, offensive exaggerations.

We've all heard them, of course. You're aware of any number of stereotypes about certain races, from the supposed athletic prowess of African-Americans to the impressive work ethic of Asians. Distasteful? Yep. Racist? Probably. But did you also realize that there are stereotypes about men? It's true. As guys grow up and slog through the process of becoming a man— something you're knee-deep in this very moment, by the way— we tend to buy into wrong ideas about what a man should be. Those misconceptions are based on stereotypes, and the stereotypes are everywhere. You hear them at school, at home, in church, and especially in the media.

That makes things hard. As a teenager, you're at the stage in life where you're starting to leave behind the kid stuff and take on more adult personality traits and responsibilities. You're looking to established men to help you define what those characteristics are. Many of you are in luck, because you have good male role models in your lives—fathers, teachers, ministers. But some guys don't have those things, so they look elsewhere for tips on manhood. And most often, that "elsewhere" means Hollywood. Their models of masculinity are Brad Pitt, Ashton Kutcher, and Vin Diesel.

Good idea? Not so much.

A boatload of media researchers and analysts have studied

the portrayal of males on TV and in the movies, and almost all of them have come to the same conclusion: The media's portrayal of what it means to be a "real" man in our society is, well, dumb. Narrow-minded. Clueless. Basically wrong. If you're taking your cues on manliness from the entertainment world, you're probably getting the wrong idea.

So it's time for a counterattack. Time to make some corrections, to offer you a real look at what it means to be a man (which, incidentally, is the idea behind this whole book—handy, huh?). To start, let's look at a bunch of those stereotypes about guys and then discuss what's real. Time to demolish the male myths.

Myth: Guys are action heroes in disguise, bringing muscles, mayhem, and mad combat skills to every situation.

Where It Comes From: Vin Diesel movies, old Bruce Willis movies, pre-Governor Arnold Schwarzenegger movies. Actually, pretty much any movie with explosions and car chases and guys with large tattooed biceps.

The Reality: Are you kidding? If I'm ever in some situation where suddenly I have to jump a motorcycle through a plate-glass window ten stories above the ground while machine-gunning a whole gang of bad guys with European accents, all while smoking a cigarette and wearing a tight-fitting shirt that emphasizes my enormous pecs—well, the next time that's required of me is the next time I'm wetting my pants. Many guys have leadership qualities. Many guys are good at taking charge of a situation. Many guys can even be heroic. But very rarely does that heroism call for a degree in motorcycle stunt-riding.

There are plenty of other ways to be a hero. A guy can be a

hero by doing the right thing, by defending the underdog or by speaking up for some kid who's being picked on. Heroes come in all shapes and sizes. And you don't have to be impossibly ripped to be one.

Myth: Guys are violent, angry, and aggressive.

Where It Comes From: Again, movies and TV shows play a big role. So does the news media and, unfortunately, real life. More men than women have been convicted of violent crimes. Almost all school shootings have involved guys. Almost all serial killers have been guys.

The Reality: The reality is that, due to the presence of *testosterone* (a hormone that sloshes through you during puberty), guys have the potential to be more aggressive than girls. Males have up to eight times more testosterone than females, and studies have linked the presence of testosterone to aggressive behavior. And since aggression leads to violence, the most violent people in the world have been and are most likely to be male.

Woohoo.

But does that mean all guys are naturally violent? Nope. Though testosterone has been linked to aggression, there's nothing conclusive that says it's the sole cause of it. Lots of things factor into our behavior, but few of them relate to biology. They have more to do with the way we were raised, with our decision-making skills, and with our level of maturity. Just because I'm a guy doesn't mean I'm kicking your teeth in if you look at me funny. I may occasionally allow myself to get mad or angry (and there's nothing wrong with that, by the way), but because I'm mature and in control of my emotions, I can keep cool whenever necessary. Violent outbursts— whether by a kid provoked into a fight at school or a major-league ballplayer who just got beaned by a Kerry Wood fastball—are impulses that give us a choice. We can choose to let the aggression loose and give in to violence. Or, we can do the manly thing and contain those impulses. Being a man means learning self-control when it comes to our competitive and aggressive nature.

STEP TO MANHOOD #37

Learning to control your aggressive, competitive impulses.
Real men know they don't always have to fight.

Myth: Guys don't cry or show emotion.

Where It Comes From: Coaches, teachers, parents, older siblings.

The Reality: A lot of guys may be uncomfortable with the expression of any emotion that's not related to, say, your team losing the World Series, but the reality is that it's okay for guys to cry. Our culture gives us the idea that guys are allowed to show "tough" emotions like anger or rage or competitiveness while burying other emotions—like crying—that aren't as cool. We showcase the aggression and hide the vulnerability.

We're way off base. Crying doesn't make you any less manly. It doesn't make you a sissy or a wimp or whatever. In fact, girls *like* a sensitive guy.

There's just one minor problem. Did you know it's physically harder for guys to cry? No lie—there's a biological block in place that keeps guys from turning on the tears as easily as girls. It's a hormone called prolactin, which is related to tear production. Once guys hit adolescence, prolactin levels drop. So teen and adult women have much more tear-producing prolactin than guys. That's why they can get all weepy at the drop of a hat. And that's why guys are pretty much only able to cry when their dog dies, even *if* they're cool

with showing emotion. This physical difference is true among men of all cultures. Worldwide, men cry less than women.

But that doesn't mean a guy *shouldn't* cry, or that it's somehow weak for a guy to cry. Not at all. Pay close attention at the end of any championship game in sports—the Super Bowl, the World Series, the NBA Finals, the Stanley Cup—and you're guaranteed to see a bunch of world-class athletes in tears. Look at legendary Kansas City Chiefs coach Dick Vermeil, who seems to get sniffly every time he gives a press conference. Watch the Academy Awards, and you'll see some of our country's biggest movie stars shed tears. Country superstar Tim McGraw—Faith Hill's husband—sings a song that says, "I don't know why they say grown men don't cry." And the Bible says Jesus wept when his friend Lazarus died.

Guys who cry are in pretty good company.

Myth: It's not cool for guys to succeed in school.

Where It Comes From: College and pro sports, movies where the jock always gets the girl, TV shows that praise athletic guys and handsome guys while making fun of smart guys. The statistics back it up. According to a book called *Real Boys: Rescuing Our Sons from the Myths of Boyhood*, by William Pollack, guys form an overwhelming majority of students at the bottom of the class in grade point average. From elementary school to high school, guys get lower grades, on average, than girls. More girls than guys attend college. More girls than guys get master's degrees.

The Reality: Aside from your spiritual beliefs, hardly anything has a bigger impact on your life than your education. Being a good student and getting an education are major, and the most successful people in the world are guys who busted their butts to excel in school. There's no question that it's cool to be an academic stud.

Then why do guys still worry about being labeled a dork/nerd/geek/Dilbert (take your pick) if they seem too smart? It has to do with the same masculine stereotypes we've already discussed. A lot of guys mistakenly believe that being creative or intellectual is somehow a feminine trait—that it's less than manly, a highway to Wedgieville. That causes guys to slack off when it comes to homework, study, and class participation. They may refuse to answer questions to keep from being called "teacher's pet." They may feel the need to disrupt the class by acting like a class clown, or by making snarky comments from the back row. I've even known guys to brag about getting a D on a test because they thought the subject matter was stupid.

> **BIG TIP:**
>
> If you want to attend a college or university, you're gonna need good grades to get in. Higher education has no place for slackers.

In reality, it's stupid to think school doesn't matter. The education thing isn't always fun, but it's important, and it's one of those times you have to look past the here and now to the future. Getting a high-school education is the difference between a career in politics or business and a career handing out shoes at the Bowl-a-Rama. Getting a college degree is the difference between being a guy who drives for the trucking company and the guy who *owns* the trucking company. And if you want to get into college? Don't expect it to be easy if you slouch your way through high school. Unless you're a 6'11" dunking machine, universities aren't much interested in slackers.

Myth: The only thing guys are interested in is sex. And girls. And sex with girls.

Where It Comes From: You have to ask? Movies. TV shows. Men's magazines like *Maxim* or *Playboy* or *Stuff*. The locker room. The hallways at school. The parking lot. Church. And so on . . .

The Reality: Yep. Guys think about sex a lot. A *whole* lot. It's said that we males reach our sexual peak around the age of eighteen. That means your sex drive is highest as you near the end of high school, and all those years leading up to it will be accompanied by a constant heightening of your libido (which is a fun-sounding fancy word for "sex drive"). The combination of rambunctious libido and sexual peakness means guys are hugely interested in sex.

But is that all they're interested in? No way. There's more to life than libido, especially when you've decided to hold off on sex until you're married, which is a good idea (lots more on that in Chapter 9). Healthy teen guys are into a lot more things than sex. Guys think about sports and exercise pretty often (see Chapter 8). Their minds are on school and friends (check out Chapter 12). They're into church and helping others (see Chapter 14).

Here's the deal: If you find yourself having sexual thoughts-a-plenty, you're normal. Then again, if it's *not* on the brain 24-7, you're also normal. You're neither a freak, a perv, or a prude. Some guys have one-track minds, some don't.

A lot of guys like to talk about sex to get attention or to enhance their reputation, and they make it sound like girls are the core of their existence. Be aware, though—they're probably exaggerating. Any time guys bring up their sexual prowess, sexual activity, sexual experience, or sexual knowledge, they're most likely overstating everything. A guy who's had sex twice will tell you he's had it four times. A guy who claims to know all the sexual moves and positions probably read a page or two in *Cosmo* or took notes while downloading porn. Loser. Guys are masters of sexual embellishment, and as a result, it seems sex is all they're into. Don't be fooled. It ain't so.

> **BIG TIP:**
>
> Any guy who constantly runs his yap about his sexual prowess is exaggerating. Guys are masters of sexual embellishment. Don't believe the hype.

It's entirely possible to get through your teen years without giving in to sexual pressure. Lots of guys have done it, and they all know one thing: There's a lot more to being a man than letting your penis be your guide.

WAYS TO BE MANLY

The point of this chapter is simple. There are lots of ways to be a man. Real masculinity—the kind that's godly, the kind that's modeled after Jesus—isn't bound by any stereotypes of what a guy is "supposed" to be. Real men can be creative or artsy or musically inclined. Real men can be intelligent and successful in school. Real men can be nurses or teachers or ministers or chefs. Real men can have a meaningful relationship with a girl without it getting complicated by sex or romantic pressure. Real men can discuss their feelings, show compassion, and be sensitive. Real men can cry without it being a news event.

On the other hand, real men can also be lumber-jacks. They can be construction workers or pro wrestlers or football players. They can be plumbers. They can be CEOs of billion-dollar corporations. Real men can pick their teeth with chain  saws and file their nails with a belt sander and hunt Kodiak grizzlies with a handful of rocks and a box of rubber bands.

What am I trying to say? There is no one single way to be manly. And, guys, that's good news. As a teenager growing into a man, that means you can just be who you are. Even if you don't have muscles. Even if you don't have a harem of girls fainting over your every move. Even if the closest you get to the playing field is as equipment manager, you're no less a man than anyone else. You're free to be you. You can do the stuff you want to do without being worried whether it's "girly" or "gay" or "wussy." Because it's not. The only thing "girly" is a girl.

It's time to bust out of the stereotypes, guys. Be your own person. Be creative. Be real. Relax about who you are, knowing that on a daily basis God is shaping you into the man he wants you to be. Keep that at the front of your brain, and stay confident. Have fun and enjoy the ride—we'll make some stops along the way, but the final destination is manhood.

CHAPTER 2
PEER PRESSURE

There's an ancient fable about an old man, a little boy, and a donkey. Stop me if you've heard it.

The old guy is traveling with his little grandson and their donkey. They pass through a village with the man leading the donkey and the boy walking alongside. This causes a lot of chattering among the townspeople, who think the old guy is an idiot for not riding on his donkey. So to please them, Gramps climbs up on the animal's back.

They reach another town. Again, the people get upset. "Old man," they scold, "how can you make that little child walk while you ride on the donkey like a king?" So to make them happy, he climbs off the donkey's back and puts the kid up.

Next village. More mad townspeople. "What a lazy, self-ish little boy," they yell. "Why does he enjoy the ride while the poor old man has to walk?" Someone suggests that both ought to ride the donkey, so the old guys hoists himself onto the animal's back, behind his grandson.

The two of them set off for the next village, where another bunch of people get their panties in a wad. "The poor donkey!" they shout. "How cruel to make it carry two people!"

The frustrated old man is last seen staggering down the road. He's carrying the donkey.

There are three things we can learn from this story. One: You can't please everybody all the time. Two: Peer pressure makes people do wacky things. Three: If you're traveling with two people, you're gonna need two donkeys. Or better yet, a car.

WHO ARE MY "PEERS," AND WHAT'S WITH ALL THE PRESSURE?

What is peer pressure? As if you don't already know. If there's one thing teens hear about on a daily basis, it's peer pressure. From the youth dude at church to the "Say No to Drugs" assembly at school, you've no doubt heard about the dangers of following the crowd. So I promise not to beat you over the head with a bunch of stuff you've heard before. But briefly—as in nanosecond briefly—I want to cover all our bases in case you were picking your nose or something during the last assembly. So . . . quickie Q&A:

Q: *Peers? What are peers?*

A: Officially, peers are a bunch of people who share a common relationship with one another. (For instance, my peers might include authors who write books for teenage guys. Or married couples with young children. Or dorks with receding hairlines.) But for our purposes here, your peers are the rest of the teenagers you come into contact with on a regular basis. They're the guys and girls you hang with. At school. At church. On your soccer or basketball team. In band or choir. Even at work.

Q: *What is peer pressure?*

A: Peer pressure is when this group of people starts urging you to do something you might not have done otherwise. Peer pressure can be both positive and negative.

Q: *What's an example of positive peer pressure?*

A: Say you're at school and some community fancy-pants comes in to speak to your government class. And when Mr. Big Shot gets up to talk, everyone gets quiet except the two obnoxious guys in the back who keep whispering to each other about, I don't know, how hot Hilary Duff is or something. So Mr. Big Shot stands there patiently, waiting for the impolite yammering to end. Everyone in your class finally gets annoyed at the two morons, until suddenly—all at once—the whole class goes "Shhhhhhhhhhhhh!"

Startled, the morons finally shut it. The pressure for them to seal their yaps doesn't come from the teacher, but from the rest of the kids in the class—their peers. That's positive peer pressure. Good job, peers.

Q: *What's an example of negative peer pressure?*

A: Oh . . . doing drugs, having sex, drinking alcohol, being a bully, making fun of the uncool—the kind of stuff you know you shouldn't do but you do anyway in order to fit in with the crowd. The stuff you do to keep from standing out like a loser—and which you regret a few hours later. That's bad peer pressure, and you know exactly what it is.

> **THE REAL DEAL:**
>
> Peer pressure isn't just a teenage thing. Everyone in every stage of life deals with it. But for teens, peer pressure can be really hard to ignore.

Q: *Why is peer pressure such a big deal for teenagers?*

A: Lots of people tend to think that peer pressure is something only teens go through, but that's not entirely true. Adults are pressured to act and live a certain way, too, from the cars they drive to the churches they attend to the civic organizations they belong to. Everyone in every stage of life deals with some kind of outside pressure to conform. But many adults have learned to ignore peer pressure. They swat it away and never look back. But as a teenager? Not so easy. Ignoring peer pressure takes buckets of guts. Let's break out of the Q&A and figure out why that is.

WHY IT'S HARDER FOR TEENS

The problem you'll face is that you're still in the process of figuring out who the heck you are. For teens, the self-identity thing is pretty hazy. Do you know what you want to do with your life? Do you know your place in God's kingdom? Do you know what gifts you have to offer the world? Have you assembled the bits and pieces of your personality and beliefs into something that makes you confident in yourself no matter the situation?

Um, let me guess: No, No, No, and Are you kidding?

And that's okay. Nobody expects you to have everything figured out. As a teenager, you're like a Polaroid picture that's still developing. You're growing physically. You're maturing mentally. You're just now beginning to discover the nuances of your personality, whether you're

funny or smart or techie or artsy. You're figuring out the stuff you like. The stuff you dislike. The stuff you're good at. The stuff you suck at. It's a process that's just getting started when you're a teen, and during these early stages, you're gonna be confused. You're waking up in a constant state of foggy uncertainty. You're not always as confident about yourself as you want to be. You want to belong, to be accepted, to fit in.

STEP TO MANHOOD #43

Being secure in your beliefs and purpose, even if you're doing things differently than everyone else.

That's why most teenagers tend to dress the same, speak the same, wear the same styles of clothing, and groove to the same music. Because at this stage in life, you're not sure enough of yourself to be cool with being different. There's nothing wrong or sinful about that at all. It's perfectly natural.

But sometimes that desire to fit in leads guys to do stuff they wouldn't normally do on their own. Here's a hypothetical: There's this group of kids you've always thought were pretty cool. Normally, you don't really hang with the in-crowd, but for some reason you manage to strike up a conversation with one of the studs, and you get invited to a weekend party he's throwing. You're not sure what to expect, but you go anyway, because you don't want to miss the chance to be cool, right? At the party, you discover that a lot of the kids—including the guy who invited you—have scored some meth. And even though they don't specifically tell you this, you get the idea that you'll find your place in the group by cranking up along with them. So you do it. You try something you never would have tried—illicit drugs—in order to be accepted by a group of your peers.

That's generally how teens get introduced to drugs, alcohol, sex, vandalism, and violence. They don't necessarily *want* to do those things, but they think it'll help them belong. And their self-confidence—the part of the brain that helps you say "No thanks, that's not my thing" to negative peer pressure, regardless of the consequences—isn't strong enough yet for that kind of challenge.

Peer pressure isn't unique to teenagers, but it is a *much harder* battle to fight. Still, you're tough. You're strong. You're becoming older, wiser, and more mature by the second. You *can* fight it. But the decision to do so is one you have to make *now*. Hold off until you're actually in the game—confronted by real pressure—and your decision-making skills will go loopy.

Secure people—people who know who they are and what role they play in the world—don't care whether or not they're different. They only care whether what they're doing is right. Doing stupid things just because that's what everyone else is doing? Secure people think that's wack.

TOOLS FOR FIGHTING PEER PRESSURE

Well . . . the subheading above is misleading, because there really aren't that many tools to fight peer pressure. In fact, there's just one. It's the word *No*. You wanna wage war on peer pressure? Then "No" is your nuclear warhead.

There are a few things, however, you can use to back up your "No." Here they are:

➤ **Your Identity.** This is who you are as a person, as a child of God, as an intelligent guy who can make intelligent decisions. As you grow older, you'll begin to get a grasp on your identity. And as you do, you'll realize that what anyone else thinks of you doesn't mean squat. What does matter is what God thinks of you (which, if I'm reading the Bible right, is a whole freaking lot). If the Creator of the universe has accepted you— warts, scabs, and all—doesn't it seem a little doofy to sell out for the attention of some kids at school?

> **Your Beliefs.** Once you figure out what you believe, those values become a part of you. Be a man and live like they're real. If you believe that drinking beer is illegal (which it is, if you're underage) and a waste of money (it costs twice as much as soda) and nasty (the old firewater is very much an acquired taste) and something that can make you act stupid (have you ever met a cool drunk guy?), then why on earth would you do something that goes against those beliefs? Why give in to alcohol due to peer pressure? Stick to your values like a tattoo to skin.

TIPS FOR SAYING "NO"

> **A simple "No, thanks"** is all you need to beat down peer pressure. Don't freak out. Don't get all nervous. Don't act weird. Just shrug it off, tell them that's not your thing, and change the subject. Move on.

> **Don't preach.** Let's be honest. If some guy offers you a cigarette, he's actually making a friendly gesture. He's being nice. Let him down gently, and don't feel like you have to give him a point-by-point analysis about the pitfalls of smoking. Nor should you get into the whole "my body is a temple of God" theology, which pretty much only church kids understand. Don't act like a nutjob. Don't launch into a speech. Don't whip out the PowerPoint presentation. A quick, easy "nope" is all you need.

➣ **Don't make a big deal**. Seeing a trend here? When confronted with peer pressure, remember: The bigger deal you make out of saying no, the bigger it will seem to the person you're turning down. Don't cause a scene or act like some great martyr for a cause.

FOUR MORE THINGS TO REMEMBER ABOUT PEER PRESSURE

➣ **You always have a choice**. It may rarely seem that way, but no one can force you to do something you don't want to do. If you do give in to peer pressure, it's not because someone else made the decision for you. It's because you decided to waver in your beliefs and morals. Whether you make good or bad choices is entirely up to you.

➣ **You're human.** That means you're gonna make mistakes. No one's completely immune to peer pressure. Not the strongest, most confident adults, and certainly not teenagers. If you give in to negative peer pressure from time to time, don't beat yourself up. It happens to everyone. Get right with God and then get over it. But if you begin to see a pattern in your behavior—if you find yourself regularly doing stuff you later regret, like breaking the law or hurting yourself or others—then you need to step up and admit you have a problem. Talk to an adult about it.

➣ **People respect a non-follower.** This is one of those things most guys don't figure out until high school's over, but when you look back, some of the people you'll remember and admire will have been the ones doing their own thing. It's easy to be a

brainless tool and follow whatever the crowd's doing. It's harder to be your own person, to be comfortable with who you are and to not care what anyone else thinks. The guys who get the most respect post-graduation are the ones who refused to let other people dictate their lives. To put it simply, the drinkers respect the guy who refuses to drink. The smokers respect the guy who thinks it's dumb to smoke. And although you'll never hear them say it, the sex-hogs respect the virgin. Why? Because they realize you're nobody's doormat.

➤ **NOT everybody's doing it**. If you listen to the media or school presentations or even if you read books like this (thanks, by the way), you may get the idea that every single person between the ages of twelve and eighteen is out having premarital sex, with a Marlboro in one hand and a Coors Light in the other. The truth is, most teens don't smoke or do drugs. Not everyone's gettin' some on the weekends. In fact, most teens make good choices most of the time. Here are some facts and figures you should be aware of:

➤ 25 percent of current seventeen- and eighteen-year-olds are smokers, according to the American Lung Association. Which means three out of four teens *don't* smoke.

➤ 52 percent of teenagers had at least one drink of alcohol in the thirty days prior to participating in a teen drinking survey by the Centers for Disease Control. Which means almost half of your peers are *not* currently drinking.

➤ Six out of ten teens surveyed by the Kaiser Family Foundation said sexual activity for high-school-age teens is *not* acceptable even if precautions are taken against pregnancy and sexually transmitted diseases. The vast majority of teens—87 percent—said it shouldn't be a big deal for teens to admit they're virgins. Most of your peers are *not* out having sex. And even when they are, they think abstinence is okay.

I won't lie to you. Peer pressure is a big deal, and it's hard to stand up to it. I gave in a time or two when I was a teenager. I've given in to peer pressure as an adult. It's tough to be so confident enough in yourself you can toss off a "no thanks" and be done with it. It's a struggle to get to the point where it doesn't matter what some dope thinks of you. But you can do it. Guys like you stand up for themselves on a daily basis, and you know what? Though it may seem you'll be rejected for not giving in to the pressure, it's usually the other way around. When some guy pressures you to drink or smoke, and you tell him no? He'll probably feel bad for asking. He won't be thinking what a dork you are. Instead, he'll be embarrassed that he's doing whatever it is in the first place. The truth is that most guys try to get someone else to follow along because they don't want to be the only one doing it. Leave them alone with their beer or smoke, and they'll feel weird about it. Peer pressure runs both ways.

When it comes to peer pressure, the trick is to say no to the negative kind, and to be one of the pressure-makers for the positive kind.

CHAPTER 3
COMMUNICATION

How many times has this happened? You have a bad day at school. Maybe it's an exam you weren't prepared for. Maybe you embarrassed yourself at soccer practice. Maybe some of the guys embarrassed you in front of a girl you like. Whatever the case, by the time last period ends, you're angry, hurt, and frustrated. You get home, storm through the front door, and sling your backpack down the hallway. You rip off your coat and chuck it into the closet, slamming the door in the process. Your dog whimpers and hides under the kitchen table.

You get to your room and kick off your shoes in frustration. They thud against the wall. By this time Mom has noticed. She's thinking about hiding under the kitchen table, but decides you might need to talk.

She's right. By the time there's nothing left to throw or kick, you're so worked up you slap your hand as hard as you can against the wall (which, on the knuckle-breakage scale, is a much better choice than punching a wall). You don't see it, but Mom flinches. Then she taps on your door, very very softly.

"You okay?" she asks.

You don't answer. Your palm is still throbbing from the hand-to-wall combat.

"You seem upset. Wanna tell me about it?"

"I'm fine."

"You didn't look fine when you came in the door."

"I'm fine. It's nothing."

"You'll feel better if you tell me what's wrong."

Everything bubbles to the surface and you explode: "LEAVE ME ALONE, MOM! I SAID I'M FINE!"

And with that, you've successfully ended the conversation, ratcheted up your tension level, lost an opportunity to spill your guts and—one more thing—you've broken your mother's heart.

This kind of scenario occurs all the time. It's one of those "Big Dumb Myths of Manhood" we hit on in the first chapter—the idea that guys are closed up as tightly as soup cans. Guys don't share. Guys don't discuss their feelings. Guys don't become vulnerable or show emotion. That stuff is for girls.

At some point in time, our culture bought into the idea that the goal of manliness was to become the strong, silent type: A man's man is never vulnerable, a man's man never shows weakness or pain. (Our parents and teachers and coaches reinforce this, by the way, when they say stuff like "Shake it off" when we hurt ourselves in a game.) So guys tend to seal themselves off from the world emotionally—we show the same cold, hard, invulnerable robot persona no matter what happens.

THE PROBLEM: TWO THINGS WE FORGET

The problem is that we fail to remember two major things. Number one, we forget that robots don't have many friends. Humans were made to connect with each other. People were designed for relationships, whether they are the family kind between parents and children, the buddy kind between guys and their friends, or the romantic kind between guys and girls. But without vulnerability, relationships can't grow. If I refuse to let out any significant, deep information—if I won't answer questions like "What's wrong?"—then you'll never get to know me. Without that knowledge, we can't develop much of a relationship. And without deep relationships, our lives will never be as full as they could have been. We'll never be able to live the complete, purposeful lives God desires for us.

Number two, we forget that Jesus was vulnerable. He was completely helpless, naked and alone when he died on the cross. He was completely helpless, naked, and practically alone when he came into the world as a baby in a manger (a feeding trough) in a barn. That's why he annoyed the Pharisees and other religious people so much—he was too vulnerable for them. He didn't act like they wanted him to. When they thought of the promised Messiah, they dreamed of a powerful ruler who would put all the enemies of God in their place.

Instead, they got a powerless baby in a barn.

Have you ever been in a barn? Have you ever *smelled* a barn? Barns are nasty, full of poop and urine and animal gunk. It's no place for a Messiah. It's no place for God.

Have you ever been around a baby? A baby is weak and dependent on someone else for everything. To feed him. To keep him

> **THE REAL DEAL:**
>
> Without vulnerability, relationships can't grow. If you refuse to answer questions like "what's wrong?" then no one will ever get to know you.

warm. To help him sleep. To keep him from, um, making a doody in his pants.

But that's where and how God decided to show his human face—in a nasty place, as a helpless baby. You can't get any more vulnerable than that.

ANKLE-DEEP IN THE KIDDIE POOL

So building relationships and becoming Christlike have something in common: vulnerability. Unfortunately, most guys aren't too good at the vulnerability thing. Like the situation above between a mom and her son, we tend to clam up when the going gets rough. We keep our feelings to ourselves. But those hidden emotions—our dreams, our desires, our worries, the things that hurt us, the things that bring happiness—are what make us who we are. They're the core of our personality.

So when we guys feel the need to hide this stuff behind a mask of "being strong," then we're actually hiding *ourselves*. Our friends only know our quiet, outside self. Our parents only know the sullen kid who refuses to ever talk about his problems. Girls never see more to us than "strength"—or whatever—and silence. They *like* both of those things, to a degree, but girls also know that a relationship requires much more than that. It requires depth. Girls want a relationship like the deep end of an Olympic-sized swimming pool. But a guy who can't communicate is only offering her one of those little plastic grocery-store baby pools, the kind with cartoon frogs and a built-in slide, because he's too focused on being manly. All he's *really* doing is turning into a surface-level guy

> **BIG TIP:**
>
> Girls want a relationship like the deep end of the swimming pool. But a guy who can't communicate is only offering her a dinky plastic kiddie pool

who can't connect with anyone—and who won't allow anyone to connect with him.

It's hard to impress the girls if you're hanging out in a purple plastic kiddie pool.

Solid communication is the backbone of any good relationship, and guys have become really lousy at building relationships. So below I'm going to give you some advice on how to communicate—how to start building healthy relationships—with the two most important kinds of people in your life today. The first are your parents. (Yeah, I know . . . *woo!* Try to keep it down.) The second is the opposite sex. Girls. Because if guys aren't sure how to communicate with the alien life forms we call our parents, then we're *really* screwed when it comes to talking with girls.

FOUR THINGS YOU SHOULD KNOW ABOUT COMMUNICATING WITH YOUR PARENTS

1. Dishonest Answers Are Never Allowed

What's a dishonest answer? A dishonest answer is when your mom asks what's wrong and you reply, "Nothing." A dishonest answer is saying, "I'm fine" when you're anything but fine. An authentic, vulnerable guy will take a deep breath and let Mom know that, yeah, something is wrong. You don't even have to go into all the gory details. It's enough to just tell her, for instance, that you got majorly embarrassed today. Or that you wrecked on a test. Or you tripped and made a stooge of yourself in front of a couple of cheerleaders. She doesn't need to know everything, but she needs to know why you came home from school in a backpack-slinging frenzy.

Be honest. Honesty builds trust. If Mom or Dad knows you're shooting them straight—that you're opening up to them about personal stuff—then they're more likely to trust you more. They'll loosen the reins a little. They'll give you more freedom. Why? Because they *know* you better.

2. Your Parents Are Weird, but They Can Relate Better Than You Think

Hard as it is to believe, your dad was once your age. Don't think too long about it—like staring at the sun, it could make you go blind—but your dad used to deal with acne and teasing and girls and wet dreams. Maybe your mom wrecked the car a time or two, or struggled with homework, or dealt with relationship problems. Your parents are real people, and they've been through the same problems you've been through. Of course, things were a *little* different back then. The world was dot-com-free. No instant-messaging. No PlayStation. MTV was new when your parents were in school, and it actually played a lot of music videos. (No, seriously.)

But even though the culture has changed, the problems you're going through aren't so different. School stuff. Girl stuff. Locker room stuff. Feeling like a dork. Feeling lost. Not fitting in. The parentals have dealt with it all before, and they somehow got through it. Don't you think they want to help you get through it, too? The easy, cop-out thing to do is to shut your parents out because you've decided they don't understand. Fine. Do it if you want. But be a man about it first. Give them a chance to prove themselves. You may be surprised.

3. Heavy Loads Are Meant to Be Shared

You know how eighteen-wheeler semis pull trailers with two rear-drive axles at the back? Each of those axles has a double set of wheels—two per side. The extra axle and wheels help keep the nearly eighty thousand pounds of cargo weight from collapsing the trailer. A long time ago, engineers decided that the only way to keep the truck moving was to distribute that weight among multiple axles and multiple tires.

Have you cracked that nutty metaphor yet? Guys like you and me carry a lot of emotional weight around. Heavy loads. Monster burdens. Most of us guys will try to handle those burdens by themselves because we think we're tough. We think we can control any situation. Problem is, we're just one axle. And some problems are so huge they can shatter a single axle into pieces. What we need is that second axle and some extra wheels.

That's where Mom and Dad come in. Expert psychologists say that just the act of bringing a problem out into the open is often all you need to get through it. Talking it over gets the situation, whatever it may be, off your shoulders and onto those of someone else. It helps you share the weight. Your parents may freak you out in general, but trust me—they'll gladly take any burden you want to hand over to them, because they love you so much. Stop gagging.

4. Communication Can Be Stress Relief

This one's related to the tip above. When you let someone else  help bear your burdens, you also practice stress relief. Think about a balloon. It's designed to handle a certain amount of air, and with each puff the balloon gets bigger.

But once it reaches the point where it's filled to capacity, any little puff has the potential to pop the balloon in a sudden burst of violence. Balloons have a pressure limit. You can't just keep adding to it without first letting a little air out. Otherwise—*bang*. Communicating is our way of "letting out air." (No, that's not a fart joke.) Life is constantly filling us with different stresses, whether they're related to school or dating or sports or work. If never released, all these pressures can keep building until we pop. I've known guys who have punched through walls, kicked through doors, and even wrecked their cars because they had so much pent-up stress inside them.

Every time you discuss a problem with your parents, it lets out a little of the stressful air. Guys can be naturally aggressive. And when stress levels get high, that aggressiveness can switch to rage, and rage is dangerous. Communicating when problems arise is a great way to keep the balloon from bursting.

HOW DO I DO IT?

Well . . . talking to your parents about hard stuff can be weird. Depending on the subject, you might feel embarrassed. You'll definitely feel uncomfortable. Don't worry, though, because it'll make your parents uncomfortable, too. To begin, give Mom or Dad some advance warning. Ask, "Can we talk about something later tonight?" This will give both of you time to gather your thoughts.

Second, admit you're nervous. Tell them it gives you the willies to talk about personal stuff. This will break the ice a little. It's honest, and your parents will appreciate that. They'll be able to relate, too—they're probably wigging about the discussion as much as you are.

Finally, take the plunge. Now that you're sitting down face-to-face with your parents, this is no time to beat around the bush, hedge your bets, or perform any other cliché that involves not being completely open and honest. Go ahead and spill your guts, because this is the perfect time. Whatever the problem—from something relatively minor that happened today at school to a fear that your girlfriend might be pregnant, which is big-time—talking with your parents about it will only deepen your relationship with them. They'll trust you more. You'll feel closer to each other. And your burden will be shared.

> ## STEP TO MANHOOD #61
>
> Actually treating your parents like real people by having an adult discussion with them.

FOUR THINGS YOU SHOULD KNOW ABOUT COMMUNICATING WITH GIRLS

1. To Be a Good Communicator, Ask Questions

Here's a *conundrum*, which is a fancy word for a weird problem, a mystery wrapped in an enigma and smothered with secret sauce. The conundrum is that everyone likes to talk about themselves, but no one likes to *listen* to people talk about themselves. And the reason we don't like to listen to someone talk about themselves is because we're so antsy to turn the conversation back to what's important: us. Humans rank high on the Me-Me-Me-O-Meter.

But that's good, because it makes conversation easy, even for shy guys. All you have to do is ask questions and listen to the answers. Open-ended questions—the kind requiring more than simple yes or no responses—are the foundations of good communication.

So what kinds of questions do you ask? Whether you're on a date, on the phone, or just hanging out in the hallway before class, try the following:

> Have you lived here all your life? ("Here" being the town you live in, as opposed to, for instance, the school hallway. Try to keep up, bonehead.)

> Tell me about your family. Do you have any brothers or sisters?

> Do you like your classes?

> Did you see (name of a recent movie or TV show)? What did you think about it?

> What are you planning to do after you graduate? Any ideas?

> Have you ever traveled anywhere?

> What did you do last weekend?

> How's your week going? Or, if it's the weekend: How was your week?

> And so on . . .

Keep in mind that, depending on the answers to any of the above, you can ask follow-up questions. When you ask her if she's ever traveled anywhere, and she answers "Chicago," then ask her about Chicago. Has she ever been to a Cubs game? Does the big city freak her out? Was it cold? Hot? Windy? Were the people friendly? That kind of thing. Ask questions, then let her answers dictate the rest of the conversation.

2. Listen

God gave us two ears and only one mouth for a reason—it's better to listen than to run your yap for hours on end. When you ask a girl a question, allow her time to answer. More important, don't interrupt her answer to turn the focus back to yourself. Here's a brief example of what NOT to do:

> **Steve**: So, have you ever traveled anywhere?
>
> **Sally**: Yeah. My family went to Chicago last summer. *(Good job so far, Steve.)*
>
> **Steve**: Did you go to a Cubs game?
>
> **Sally**: No. We tried to. My dad wanted to see if there were any tickets, so we rode the Red Line to Addison near Wrigley, and then—
>
> **Steve**: Man, I'd give anything to go to Wrigley. I *love* the Cubs. I've been watching them on TV since I was little, back with Ryne Sandberg and Andre Dawson and Harry Caray, and my brother used to always blah blah blah blah blah . . . *(Oooohhhh . . . you lose, Steve. Go home and punch a wall.)*

A woman likes nothing better than a guy who is interested in what she has to say. And nothing is more obnoxious than a guy who can only talk about himself. Worse still is the guy who keeps talking about his last girlfriend, or about what he and his buddies did last weekend. The key to male-female communication is to be polite, take the focus off yourself, and listen. And don't just *pretend* to listen while thinking up your next question, but *really* listen. Attentively. There's a difference, and—trust me—she can pick up on it.

> **BIG TIP:**
>
> Shut your piehole and listen. Nothing is more obnoxious than a guy who thinks the only thing worth talking about is himself.

3. Remember Body Language

Back in third grade, this girl named Hayden once told me she knew three languages: English, Pig Latin, and *body* language. And with that, she put her hands on her hips and swayed them around suggestively. I had no idea what she was talking about. Utterly clueless. On the other hand, Hayden was weird.

Of course, I was, like, seven at the time, so my ignorance can be excused. But as a teenager, you need to be aware of body language, because girls your age most certainly are. The most important thing to show her through body language is that you're interested in what she has to say. Some tips:

> ➤ **Lean forward slightly.** Slouching indicates boredom. Leaning back too far appears overconfident and cocky.

> ➤ **Make eye contact.** There's nothing that says "I could care less about what you're saying" than staring out the window when someone's talking to you. If you don't know the color of her eyes by the end of the conversation, you're doing it wrong.

➤   **Smile**. Duh.

➤   **Don't fidget.** Many people assume fidgetiness is a sign
of discomfort or nervousness or even boredom. If you're
bouncing your foot throughout the entire conversation,
she'll assume you're eager to be done with it. That's not
always true, of course—sometimes guys are just bursting with energy, and squirminess is a way to release it—
but do your best to keep it to a minimum.

➤   **Don't cross your arms, frown, yawn, or look at
your watch.** Each of these physical gestures can indicate
disapproval or a lack of interest. Steer clear of these until
the conversation's over.

HOW DO I DO IT?

Back into Honest Abe Mode—a lot of guys have trouble
communicating with girls. Guys don't really talk to each other
very much, unless it's about sports or video games or something cool we saw on TV. We're inexperienced conversational-
ists. We're not into the stuff girls are interested in. We're
afraid they'll think we don't have anything interesting to say.
We're afraid to get into anything personal or deep. As I've
already mentioned, oh, once or twice in this chapter, we're losers at communication.

That's why asking questions and listening attentively are
the two key things you should do when it's time to engage the
opposite sex in conversation. Get her talking and pay attention
to what she says, and you'll be well on your way to relationship-building. It won't be as hard as you might think, but

remember this: At some point, the conversation will turn. *She'll* begin asking the questions, and *you're* gonna have to talk. About yourself. About how you *feel*.

You'll do fine, of course. Just remember that time is coming.

CHAPTER 4
DATING

So, you've taken all the advice from the previous chapter about communicating with girls. You're starting to feel a little more comfortable hanging with the opposite sex. You're thinking maybe you're beginning to connect with a certain girl in particular. You find yourself sliding into that daydreamy kind of thought pattern, playing a mental "what would it be like" game. What would it be like to hold hands with her? What would it be like to rent a movie and cuddle up on the couch? What would it be like to kiss her?

And before you know it, you're a little bit interested—okay, a *lot* interested—in someone. You're ready to ask her out, ready to go on a real date and everything. And as someone who has been there, let me be the first to tell you there is nothing more exciting and terrifying all at the same time than that first date between a guy and a girl who are starting to like each other.

That crushed-out anticipation is one of the best feelings in the world, and it's fairly unique to teens. It's one of the aspects of teenagerdom that can make the years between twelve and eighteen some of the most exhilarating of your life—the flirting and talking and eye contact and fleeting touches that develop from an initial spark into a real-life, dating relationship. We'll discuss this in much greater detail in Chapter 9 (if you haven't done so already, check out "The Sex Chapter," starting on page 91), but

38

when it comes to dating, it's important to understand that God created us to connect with members of the opposite sex. He noticed in the Garden of Eden that it was "not good for the man to be alone" (Genesis 2:18), so he whipped up a recipe for Eve out of one of Adam's ribs. *Bam!* The first couple. Guys and girls were made for each other.

God intends meaningful, caring, and even romantic relationships with members of the opposite sex. The ultimate expression of that design is for one of those relationships to become deeper, more caring, and more fulfilling than any of the previous ones—at which point it plunges into marriage. (Marriage is also when God intends the romantic aspect of the relationship to take a mega-plunge of its own—into a *sexual* relationship. Somebody give me an "amen.") As guys grow older, we start to crave an emotional and physical connection with girls, and that desire usually morphs into dating relationships.

STEP TO MANHOOD #8

Your first honest-to-goodness girlfriend.

Which brings us to the cold hard truth: Very few junior-high or high-school romances last. As in, *maybe* one out of a hundred. Most teenage relationships don't turn into anything long-term. But they can be extremely serious. They can involve commitment and intense emotions and even love. But odds are they'll never be more than nice memories you'll put aside once you meet the girl of your dreams.

That's why it's best to view dating as an opportunity to have fun and learn the rules in a relatively safe environment.

SPEAKING OF SAFE ENVIRONMENTS, WHAT ABOUT COURTSHIP?

Dating is a fairly new cultural phenomenon. Nobody really dated—as we define it—until the twentieth century rolled around. Before then, families would kind of act as a dating service for their kids, with Mom and Dad helping to choose a potential mate. Yeeesh. Guys and girls wouldn't hardly get involved at all until they were both ready for marriage, to each other. No dating. No movies. Just a brief period of betrothal/engagement and then the wedding bells began to clang.

And now, a century later, some Christians are calling for a return to a similar process. It's called courtship, and it means that guys and girls get together—with their families' permission and involvement—solely for the purpose of getting married. Let's say a guy and girl start to click. They then proceed to build a friendship in a safe, non-dating, non-making-out environment. Without the physical stuff and emotional complexity to confuse them, they put their relationship in God's hands and focus on each other as potential life partners. Then, once the foundation of friendship is laid, they move straight into marriage. There's no dating involved. No traditional engagement. They do not pass "Go." This courting relationship is intended to be the only romantic relationship each person has before marriage—with no physical or emotional intimacy allowed, until the honeymoon—and it's chaperoned throughout by the couple's parents.

Again—and not to be disrespectful—*yeeesh*.

Wait. I shouldn't knock the idea of courtship, because the folks behind it make some good points. There's nothing wrong with serious relationship-building, and there's nothing

wrong with parental involvement. Christians who advocate
courtship before marriage
believe it's more biblically
sound than dating. They think
it gives you a better chance at
remaining premaritally pure.
They see it as a way to flee sexual temptation. They also

> **THE REAL DEAL:**
> One problem with casual
> dating is that it's so easy to
> break things off when it
> doesn't work out. Some say
> this makes it a training
> ground for divorce.

worry that it's too easy to develop excessively strong emotional attachments on the teen dating scene, and too easy to
just break things off if it doesn't work out. The "breaking up
and moving on" aspect of casual dating can lead to psychological trauma and may even be a way to "practice" for
divorce. That ain't good.

Another concern the courtship camp has is that dating can
be a selfish activity. Sure, guys and girls go out because they
enjoy one another's company. But they're also looking for the
minor titillation physical contact brings. What begins as handholding and hugging and kissing can easily turn into more illicit stuff. They argue that dating relationships make it too easy to
give in to the intense physical pressures of the sex drive. And I'll
be the first to say it: They're right.

My feeling is that as teenagers, guys and girls are inevitably
gonna get involved with each other. Guys are attracted to girls.
Girls are attracted to guys. Both are curious. Both want to develop
more meaningful relationships with the opposite sex without all
the pressure of marriage. And for teenagers? That's okay. The
trick is to develop those meaningful relationships (and, eventually, to break them off) without hurting each other in the
process. *And* while staying pure.

THE TEN COMMANDMENTS OF DATING

Here, then, are the rules of dating for Christian guys, intended to help you navigate the choppy waters of love without going too far physically, without falling into a gut-wrenching breakup, and while trying to follow Jesus in all you do. Like a lot of cultural stuff, there is no "dating verse" or chapter in the Bible to give us much direction. There is no dating in the Bible, period. There's lots of marriage, lots of sex, and lots of love talk, but nothing we can take home about guy-girl hanging out. What we *can* do is consider some key biblical principles and apply them to the modern dating scene, with a few practical suggestions thrown in for good measure. With that in mind, then, here are your Ten Commandments of Dating, in no particular order:

1. Treat Her with Respect at All Times

Whenever you go on a date, you absolutely must keep one thing in mind: *This girl will one day become someone's wife.* Maybe the two of you will hit it off, defy the odds, and eventually marry each other. Or more likely, she'll fall in love with someone else a few years down the road. Whatever the case, when you go out, you've been given the privilege of spending quality time with someone's future wife. That means treating her with the utmost care and respect. Enjoy the time you have together, but also keep an eye on the future. Don't do anything with her you wouldn't want someone else doing with *your* future wife.

> **BIG TIP:**
>
> Your date is probably someone else's future wife. Don't do anything with her you wouldn't want someone else doing with your future wife.

2. Treat Her Parents with Respect

This means you never never never just drive up to her house, honk the horn, and wait for her to come outside. Instead, park the car and go to the door. Meet her parents. Give them the chance to meet you, to discover what a great guy you are, and to develop trust in you. Tell them your plans for the evening, including where you're going and when you'll have their daughter home. Then keep your word. Remember, you're taking their daughter out, and nothing is scarier to a parent than their angel getting in a car with some drooly teenage guy. *Nothing.* Show them respect and you'll soothe some of that fear. They're putting a huge amount of trust in you. It's your job to live up to it.

3. Give Her a Reason to Respect You

How? By taking things slowly. For some guys (and girls), dating is just an excuse to get alone and start playing tongue darts. That can be fun, but it's not the purpose of dating. The purpose of dating is to develop deeper relationships with the opposite sex. Get to know her. Ask questions. Be interested. Find out her middle name. Figure out the color of her eyes. Discover what she wants to do after graduation. And when the date is over and you're wondering whether you can get away with a good-night kiss? Take all the guesswork out of it and do the respectful thing: Ask her for permission. Seriously. You'll feel like a dork, but she'll be very impressed. Because you have shown respect for her, she'll respect you back. And if she says yes, that'll be one great kiss. *(Important note: Just so you'll know, there is no rule that says a date must end in a kiss. None. At. All. Got it? Paying for dinner is no guarantee of a smooch—or anything else. Never forget that.)*

4. Compliment Often

She'll probably look great. She probably *always* looks great, but make sure you let her know. There's no better way to start a date than by making her feel attractive and special. And guys? Make sure you compliment her in a *respectful* way. There's a major difference between "That outfit looks great on you" and "When I look at you in that dress, all's I'm thinkin' is 'Nice rack!'" Please. Keep your pants on, Cyrano.

5. If Possible, Date in Groups

The best way to get to know someone initially is in a group-dating situation. A table for eight isn't ideal for deep, intimate conversation, but it *does* give you the chance to develop a relationship in a nonthreatening atmosphere. Group dating keeps the chatter flowing, and it helps you avoid any tempting situations. Speaking of which . . .

6. Avoid the "Hanging Out at Home" Date Like the Plague

Anything done at home—especially home alone—is a recipe for physical/sexual disaster. You may have just intended to rent a movie and share a bowl of popcorn, but who's to say you won't end up with popcorn all over the couch and your hands in places they shouldn't be? Unless you're playing Scrabble with her parents, dating at home should be avoided at all costs.

7. Don't Go to a Movie, Either

While dinner and a movie may be the standard date, it's hardly ideal. Dinner is fine, but how much getting to know one another are you going to accomplish during a movie? It's dark, you can't talk, and there are lots of distractions—for instance, *the movie.* Find something else to do, especially at the beginning of

> **BIG TIP:**
>
> Movies are not an ideal environment for a date, because they're terrible places to attempt a conversation.

a relationship when good conversation is a must. *(Check out the list below for ideas on fun and creative dates.)*

8. Stay Away from Danger Zones

And by danger zones, I don't mean the parts covered by her swimsuit. (Though that's also a good rule.) I mean situations where things can get out of control. The previously mentioned "stay-at-home date" is one danger zone. Another is the party scene. Parties aren't bad in themselves—sometimes they fit within the group-dating ideal—but occasionally you can end up with a bunch of people who don't share the same values as you and your date. Many parties are just well-attended excuses to get drunk or get high or get some, sexually speaking. You can be sure there will be lots of pressure to kick the physical stuff up a notch with your date—stuff that goes way beyond "spin the bottle." Any combination of partying, drinking, and bottle-spinning is no place to be hanging out with someone's future wife. Danger zone. Got it?

9. Date to Give, Not to Receive

It's the golden rule, you know: Do unto others as you would have them do unto you. And as a Christian, this should be your attitude on the dating scene. Are you in it to boost your self-esteem? To get the adrenaline boost flirtation brings? To get some action? Or are you in it to get to know another person, to enjoy her company, to make sure she has a nice evening? One of the keys to a successful relationship—*any* relationship—is to be a giver, not a taker. Give her compliments, give her flowers, give her your attention. Give her the chance to talk about herself. Give her the choice of restaurants or activities. Give her your best. The best advice I can give you is that *it's not all about you*. And that applies to every aspect of life. Not just dating.

STEP TO MANHOOD #33

Realizing it's not all about you.

10. Date Your Equal

Thankfully, this doesn't mean only people of equal attractiveness can date each other. Because no way would I have gotten married to such a beautiful wife if that were true. Not a chance. Dating your equal means dating your *spiritual* equal. You've probably heard someone use the phrase "unequally yoked," as in, don't be yoked together with someone who doesn't believe the same as you.

In the twenty-first century, farming terms like "yoke" don't make much sense to us, so let's think of it using a different example. Let's say you're handsome, a strapping 5'10", 165 pounds, and you're in a three-legged race with a two-year-old little girl who's only been walking for a few months. The two of you? Unequally yoked. You might be able to drag her around a little, but more than likely she's going to drag *you*. As in down. It's doubtful you and the little princess will win the race. Same goes for dating. You may think it's fine to date a non-Christian because it's not like you're gonna get married or anything. You're just having fun, right? But what if you date a girl who's not interested in saving herself for marriage? What if you date a girl who's into drinking? What if you date a girl who thinks Christianity is stupid? It's hard to have a healthy relationship if the two of you aren't on the same page for the big issues. Any kind of dating relationship—even if it's just a one-time invitation to a dance—will work better if it's between two people who share the same values.

CREATIVE ACTIVITY DATE OPTIONS

As discussed earlier, a movie is not the best venue for a date, particularly a first date. The best place for a first date is anywhere that stimulates good conversation and keeps you entertained for a couple of hours. That's why lots of dating experts recommend activity dates for the first date. Next time you're planning a date—whether group or solo—consider building it around one of the following options:

BIG TIP:

One of the best ways to impress a girl is with a unique idea for a date. Dinner and a movie is so . . . expected. It's ho-hum. She deserves better.

> **Picnic** (Make sure to bring something she likes to eat.)

> **Picnic at night**, under the stars (Make sure to bring something she likes to eat, and a flashlight.)

> **Miniature golf** (Play to have fun, not to win. If you're throwing your clubs after a miss? Too competitive.)

> **Regular, non-miniature golf** (Same as above.)

> **Driving range** (Wow. You must really like golf.)

> **In-line skating** (Drawback: Elbow pads are so not attractive.)

> **Ice skating** (Runny noses? Also unattractive.)

> **Amusement park** (Win her a stuffed animal!)

> **Ping-Pong or pool** (Again, go easy on the competitiveness.)

> **Hiking** at a nearby state park or nature center (Try not to get lost.)

> **Tennis** (Just because "love" is part of the game.)

> **Basketball** (Try a game of H.O.R.S.E. Do not attempt to school her with your dunking prowess.)

> **Visit a local museum** (A little culture and refinement go a long way.)

> **Go to the zoo** (Please do not taunt the monkeys.)

> **Participate in a charity walk or run** (Exercise for a cause.)

> **Volunteer** (Build a Habitat for Humanity home or serve food at a local shelter.)

> ➣ **Attend a sporting event** (Root, root, root for the home team.)

> ➣ **Visit a flea market** (Buy her something weird, cheap, and unexpected.)

FINAL WORDS OF ADVICE

Lots of teenagers look at dating lots of different ways. Some guys jump from girlfriend to girlfriend, committing themselves to that special someone every few months or so. They put the moves on a hottie, plant a well-timed kiss or two, then enjoy several weeks of relationship-building and, um, physical gratification—then they drop her like a hot biscuit and move on to the next one. Don't be that guy. That guy is selfish. Jerk's making a catch, using her for her body, then leaving her in a bunch of shattered pieces.

Some guys do more than jump from girl to girl—they bounce. A lot. Constantly moving and never committing, the game they're playing is flirtation. They flirt to get attention. They flirt to boost their ego. They flirt because of the adrenaline rush it gives them. They flirt up to the edge, then they move in for a little action. These are the guys who hook up with a girl one night at a party, engage in a little make-outage (or more), then forget the girl the next day. Don't be this guy, either. He's a user and a tease. He's just as selfish, if not more, because he's after the thrill with none of the commitment. He doesn't even *pretend* to commit. Dude's a slut.

Some guys are talkers. They don't date much, but they want you to think they do. They make sure you know every move they've ever made on a girl. They're the seniors at the Winter

Dance pawing some cute, unsuspecting freshman, just for the appearance of it, so everyone will notice their conquest. They date to be seen. They kiss and tell. Sometimes they just tell. These guys are after the reputation, thinking a ladies' man rep will help them score dates. They want to be known as studs. Don't be this guy. He's not just a moron, he's an *obnoxious* moron. (And according to most women I've talked to, he's dead wrong. Girls don't want to be one of many.)

But some guys, thankfully, are gentlemen. They date for several reasons. One, they like girls (who doesn't?). Two, they realize that dating is about deepening friendships. Occasionally they find a friend they'd like to get to know better, so they come up with fun and safe things for the two of them to do together. Three, they know that dating as a teenager is a way to test the waters of relationships. It's practice for the real thing somewhere down the road.

Guys like this are always respectful of both the girl and her parents. They realize that sex is special—something God approves of once you're married, but not before—so they're not trying to put the moves on or anything. They're satisfied with a meaningful kiss and a little handholding. They like the conversation and companionship. They like having someone to talk to about deep stuff, like faith and fears and the future. They realize that what happens on a date isn't for the world to know, that their buddies don't need all the details. They never act like their date owes them anything. They don't ever take advantage. They are romantic and thoughtful and are in it for reasons other than pleasing themselves.

That's the kind of guy you want to be: a gentleman. Lucky for you, that's what the whole next chapter is about. Keep reading.

CHAPTER 5

THE NEXT-GENERATION GENTLEMAN

Pop Quiz

You're approaching a department store door at the same time as a woman in her early thirties. You reach the door first. What do you do?

a. Open the door and march right on in ahead of her.

b. Open the door and allow her to enter ahead of you.

c. Pretend to tie your shoe until she opens the door herself and makes it through safely.

d. It depends: What store are we talking about?

Being a man in the twenty-first century can be confusing, because our society's concept of how men are supposed to act keeps changing. Should we be the manly, aggressive *Fight Club* kind of guys? Should we be sensitive, hair-gelled, moisturizer-slathering metrosexuals? Are we expected to pick up the tab on a date? Should we open the doors for women or not? The rules and expectations, it seems, are constantly shifting. It wasn't always this hard.

Back in the 1800s, the world was a different place. Not necessarily better, mind you, just different. This was before the feminist movement had given women the opportunity to do

51

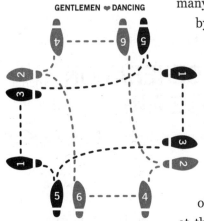

GENTLEMEN ♥ DANCING

START

many things traditionally done by men—things like run for political office, become doctors or lawyers or CEOs of corporations, or even vote in elections. (Amazingly, women weren't allowed to vote until 1920! See? That's what I mean by "not necessarily better.") Regardless of how backward society was at the time, one good thing the 1800s had going was that gender roles were simpler. Most men had a pretty good idea of who they were and what they were supposed to do.

They were supposed to be gentlemen.

What was a gentleman? Here's a good description of the term, taken from a book published in 1886 called *Rules of Etiquette and Home Culture*: "It is the duty of a gentleman to know how to ride, to shoot, to fence, to box, to swim, to row and to dance. He should be graceful. If attacked by ruffians, a man should be able to defend himself, and also to defend women from their insults."

I've never personally been attacked by ruffians, and I'm guessing you haven't, either. In fact, I'm not sure I'd recognize a ruffian if one came up and smacked me in the nose—much less would I be able to defend myself should that occur. Even worse, I'm not a great rider, unless you count bicycles. Shooting and fencing? Not so much. I've never boxed. I can swim pretty well. I once rowed a kayak at summer camp, and I was a fairly decent break dancer back in the day. So, according to the standards above, I guess I'm a half-gentleman.

FEMINISM MADE THINGS TRICKY

Today, the term "gentleman" seems a little, well, old-fashioned. When guys hear it, they may think of a tuxedo-wearing James Bond type who opens the door for a woman, who stands when a woman enters the room, and who pulls the chair out for her and pushes it back in. Such behavior has its roots in the Middle Ages. Back then, it was called *chivalry*, a concept that described the ideal behavior of a knight who dedicated his life to serving his king and protecting his lady. A more modern opening-doors-for-women form of chivalry was generally expected of men up until the 1960s and 1970s, at which time people started to really question some of the hidden attitudes behind the gentlemanly ideal—namely that women were weaker than men, and that they somehow needed to be protected and taken care of. (Thus, their perceived inability to open doors for themselves.)

In the 1950s, there was pretty much one career option for women: Stay home and be a mom and loving housewife. In the 1960s, women began demanding more from society. They wanted to be treated equally. They wanted to be given the same chances to succeed as men. They wanted to have the same jobs, the same pay, and the same responsibilities. They were no longer content to be quiet, cookie-baking domestic helpers for their breadwinning husbands.

These then-radical ideas gave birth to a movement called *feminism* in the 1970s, the main focus of which was the idea that women were equal to men. No longer were they inferior, helpless, or in need of protection. This was a good thing, because it gave moms the opportunity to break out from gender stereotypes. Now they were free to pursue their dreams and make a difference in the world, when otherwise they wouldn't have been given the chance.

But there was one less-than-positive side effect of feminism: Guys got scared. They weren't sure how to act. They still respected women and wanted to demonstrate that respect, yet many of their ways of doing that fell within the gentlemanly ideal—things like opening doors for their wives, mothers, and girlfriends. *What if,* they began asking themselves, *by opening this door, I'm somehow telling her that she's incapable of opening it herself? Will she be offended?* The entire universe of etiquette and manners began to shift. Plenty of us guys just didn't know what to do anymore, and as a result, the traditional actions of chivalry slowly started to fall away.

Until recently. Now the tide is again turning. Since September 11, people have begun to value things like politeness, respect, and good manners—but this time, with a twist. Manners maven Emily Post calls it "gender-free chivalry," and it's based on something we all learned in preschool: being kind to one another. No longer is chivalry just a case of men taking care of women. The ideal in today's world is people taking care of people.

For Christian guys, this idea comes right from the New Testament. Chapter 5 of Ephesians has been controversial because that's where Paul talks about relationships between wives and husbands. He tells wives to submit to their husbands, and husbands to love their wives as Christ loved the church. Feminists are uncomfortable with the "submit to their husbands in everything" part (Ephesians 5:24), and men aren't sure what it means when Paul says husbands are to be "head of the wife as Christ is the head of the church" (Ephesians 5:23). But one thing men and women

> **THE REAL DEAL:**
>
> The ideal in today's world is people taking care of people.

both seem to miss is a tiny verse right before the whole passage—verse 21, which says, "Submit to one another out of reverence for Christ." Submit to *one another.* Guys submit to girls. Girls submit to guys. Teenagers submit to authority figures. Authority figures submit to teens. Sound revolutionary? It is. It means, as a guy, you should treat everyone—men and women, boys and girls, toddlers and grandparents—with the same measure of respect, politeness, and kindness, regardless of who they are. You should treat people as Jesus treated people.

That's what it means to be a new-generation gentleman, and as a Christian guy you should strive to be that kind of person, even if you're still in your teens. Now that you know, let's get into the details of how to do it.

COURTLY BEHAVIOR

We'll start with the toughest category of all, the holdover gestures that men typically have performed for women. Again, these days it's acceptable for people of any gender to display this sort of kindness to anyone else—guy or girl. The following are examples of unisex manners, and a gentleman is always on the lookout for ways to put them to use:

HOLDING A DOOR OPEN

Whether it's a car door, a restaurant door, or even the door to a classroom, if you get there before a girl (or any companion), open it and hold it for her. This is an easy rule to follow, so make it a habit. People always appreciate someone who holds a door open for them, whether it's your girlfriend, your grandfather, or a stranger at the mall.

GIVING UP YOUR SEAT

If a woman of any age arrives while you're on the bus, the subway, at a table, or anyplace where chairs are scarce, stand up and offer your seat to her. She won't always accept, but the offer will be appreciated. Same goes for an elderly man.

HELPING WITH A COAT

Anyone who is struggling to put on their coat should be helped. This is especially true with senior citizens—and there's no doubt they'll enjoy the chivalry.

HELPING TO CARRY SOMETHING

Anytime someone's carrying a heavy or awkward load, it's polite to ask if you can help. They'll almost always take you up on it, unless what they're carrying is private or dangerous. (If you see someone carrying, for instance, a long-range assault rifle? Better just mind your own business, even if it looks heavy.)

PAYING FOR A MEAL

You may not be dating yet, but you will someday. If you asked the girl out, then you should pay for a meal unless you've discussed a different arrangement first. It's not uncommon for dates to split a meal or a movie, or even for the girl to pay. But the rule these days is that the host—whoever initiated the date—pays for the meal. So start saving now.

GO EASY ON THE PDA

Yeah, we know you two love each other, but we don't need to see you nibbling on her ear in the Food Court at the mall. It may seem stupid and prudish to you, but Public Displays of Affection, especially between teenagers, generally make onlookers hit 10 on the discomfort scale. People realize that guys and girls like to kiss and hug and all that—heck, I like to kiss and hug, too—but that's the kind of thing you do in private. Keep it discreet.

BASIC POLITENESS

In the grand scheme of things, you're still relatively young, so you can be forgiven for not knowing all the rules of proper behavior. In fact, *I'm* still relatively young in the grand scheme of things, and I certainly don't know all the rules. Ask me which fork goes with your salad and all you'll get from me is a shrug. I don't know that stuff. I'm no Mister Fancy Pants. Still, there are a few ground rules that show the world you weren't raised by wolves. Here are a few of the biggies, in no particular order:

LISTEN MORE THAN YOU SPEAK

Some guys can't keep their mouths shut. They can't wait for you to finish talking so they can get in the last word. They interrupt. They're always turning conversations back toward themselves. They suffer from verbal diarrhea. Don't be that kind of guy. A polite person always listens first, waiting for another to finish talking before making a comment of his own. Failing to do so gives the not-so-subtle message that what *you* have to say is more important than what someone else has to say. Welcome aboard the ego train.

KEEP YOUR TEMPER IN CHECK

Guys are naturally more aggressive than girls, and therefore it's easier for us to lose our temper. Whether it's on the football field, at school, or after your buddy just destroyed you in a round of Madden, a gentleman always tries to keep his emotions under control. Sometimes it's impossible—even Jesus went medieval a time or two (remember the moneychangers at the temple?)—but our society has a word for guys who try to maintain control at all times: *mature.*

KEEP PERSONAL GROOMING PRIVATE

PICKIN PRIVATE

You're not a cat. Don't act like one by grooming yourself in public. Everyone has to pick their nose, pick their teeth, pop a zit, or chew on a cuticle every now and then. But those are things that should be done in private. There's nothing more disgusting than the dude gnawing on his fingernails or excavating a nostril in the middle of third period. Don't be him.

KEEP BATHROOM NOISES PRIVATE

We're all guys here, so let's be honest: Farts can be funny. But there's a time and a place, and mixed company is neither of those. Some of my friends and I used to get our kicks by letting 'em rip against our plastic chairs from the back of our sixth-grade language arts class. We did it because it made the rest of the guys laugh. But the girls didn't ever think it was quite as cool as we did. Now I realize why: We were idiots. Farts smell, farts are gross, and if you're a fine Christian gentleman, farts have no place in public situations. Same goes for belching. But at home watching the game with a few (male) friends? Bring it on, Stinky.

SPEAK GRACEFULLY

What does "verbal gracefulness" mean? It means saying things like "Pardon me" or "Sorry" when you bump into someone, step on a toe, or have to edge past a person in a tight situation. It means getting a stranger's attention by saying "Excuse me" rather than shouting "Hey!" It means always acknowledging someone the first time you meet by saying something like "Nice to meet you." It means always thanking your host at a party or after a meal. And it means complimenting people every chance you get—not just when you're trying to impress a girl.

Every guy your age—whether he expresses it or not—wants to be treated more like an adult and less like a child. Well, here's a secret: The things listed above are the sorts of refinements that mature adults are expected to know. Start practicing them now, and people will take notice. And once they take notice, they'll begin treating you more like an adult. Manners are the first stop on the road to adulthood.

FINAL THOUGHTS

A lot of guys have the wrong idea about things like etiquette, manners, and the importance of being a gentleman. Maybe they think it's an old-fashioned list of rules that keep life from being spontaneous and fun. Maybe they think good manners only come into play at a fancy dinner party or an event like the prom. Maybe they think people who are overly polite are boring and stuffy.

None of those ideas are true.

The whole backbone to the gentlemanly code is *respect*. Making good manners a part of your daily routine is simply a way of showing respect to everyone you come into contact with:

your family, your teachers, your friends, and even the weird dude behind the counter at the convenience store. And you know what? Nobody's more impressed by basic politeness than the opposite sex. Feminism may have made things confusing, but most girls these days are blown away by guys who treat them like ladies. Trust me: There's nothing more attractive to a girl than a guy who acts like a gentleman.

PART TWO
BODY

CHAPTER 6

GROOMING

Your Appearance Matters. Your appearance—the way you look and, yes, smell—is a big deal. A *very* big deal. Why else would otherwise normal people spend thousands of dollars on plastic surgery? Why else would the supermarket shelves be so full of tanning creams and diet products and hair gels? Why else would Michael Jackson look the way he does?

Nah . . . scratch the last one. That'll never be explained.

The sad truth in this day and age is that *looks matter*. The concept is miles away from the don't-judge-a-book-by-its-cover ideal, and it's certainly not what the Bible teaches, but it's true nonetheless. Painful, wrong, unfair—but the real deal in the here and now. Want proof? Over the last several years, several different scientific researchers have discovered that good-looking people (women *and* men) had significant advantages in getting job interviews, receiving job offers, keeping a job, and getting promoted. Even more discouraging are the studies that find good-looking kids do better in school.

Why? Because their teachers *expect* them to do better because they're so freaking attractive!

That stinks—and not in the spray-on deodorant kind of way. It also makes sense in a weird chain of logic. Let's follow the progression: Say you hit puberty one summer, exploding from a 90-pound shrimp to a 135-pound stud over the course of two months. Your shoulders get broader. Your voice gets deeper. Your jaw line becomes more defined. Muscles develop. You go from boy to man almost overnight.

Whoa.

Have you changed on the inside? Not really. But you're certainly aware that you look better; in fact, you can see it in the mirror. When school begins, you show up on Day One feeling a little more relaxed and a lot more confident. Thanks to the dose of confidence, your social skills perk up. You're willing to take a few more chances. Maybe you toss a self-assured smile to the hottie in the back of your algebra class. Maybe you wink at the girls who just turned their heads when you passed them in the hall—girls who wouldn't have given you the time of day last year. This bumps your confidence even more, and you go through the day spiked on a natural adrenaline high. Your senses are keener. You listen better. You remember better. You pay attention better. You process information better.

You've become a better student—your memory, attention span, and brainpower have received energy boosts—because of the confidence you gained from the psychological impact of suddenly *looking* better.

That's an extreme scenario, but research suggests there's a lot of truth to it. That's why many of the most successful

> **THE REAL DEAL:**
>
> Today's society values beauty and good looks, and attractive people sometimes seem to have it better. But you can't make it through life on looks alone.

people in our society are, incidentally, also the most attractive.

Cool? Weird? Completely unfair? Yep, it's all of those things. It's also very superficial. That's because all of us know, deep down, the way we look on the outside isn't nearly as important as who we are on the inside. In fact, in the example above, the truly beneficial stuff was what developed on the inside—increased confidence and better attention span. Appearance was the catalyst that got the party started.

That's why a pretty face won't make you rich and famous, unless you're a supermodel. That's why great hair or skin won't make you the most popular guy in school or guarantee you a spot on the varsity team. That's why colleges don't give scholarships based solely on your photograph. The way you look has to combine with other, more important things—your personality, your intelligence, your sense of humor—in order for people to get the whole picture of who you are. Appearance is only one piece of the puzzle. Unfortunately, our society stretches that single puzzle piece into a really big one.

One more biggie to remember: Good looks may boost your confidence and make you feel great for a season, but they are no guarantee of true happiness. Why do you think there are so many divorces in Hollywood? Why else do rock stars and lingerie models hook up and break up so randomly? *Pretty* doesn't equal *happy*, and anyone who buys into that lie is getting schooled by something completely shallow. Looks only scratch the surface of who you are, and that's the truth.

I'm telling you this only because we're about to get into a discussion of the importance of grooming, and grooming is the process of making yourself look good. Is it, like, the most important thing ever? No way. But is it significant? Yes. It's a major deal in life—especially the life of a teenager. Think of your appearance as a tool. It can help boost your confidence and express your personality. It can make some aspects of life easier. And, most important, it's something you control. So keep that in mind as we launch into Grooming 101.

SHAVING

You know how the buff, shiny, hairless dude in the TV commercial swipes a gleaming razor across his cheeks—just a couple of strokes is all it takes—and suddenly some hot, not-quite-fully-dressed babe starts nuzzling his baby-soft skin?

If only that were true.

It's not. Once you pick up your first blade, shaving is nothing more than an annoying ritual you have to perform after staggering out of bed in the morning. You're barely able to see because your eyes are still blurry with sleep, but nevertheless you've gotta start dragging a sharp object across your face. And you have to do it every single day of your life until you die or go all Moses with a permanent beard. Maybe it seems cool and sexy and mature the first couple of times, but just wait. That'll change.

STEP TO MANHOOD #8

Your first shave.

Every year, manufacturers come up with some new kind of shaving technology. Electric shavers that spit out moisturizing goop. Pivoting heads. Multiple blades. Patented "lift and cut" systems. You know why all these products are on the market? It's because guys are never satisfied with their shaving experience. It's always hard, and we always think it ought to be easier. As someone once said, shaving is literally a pain in the neck.

But even though it's something we do every day, a lot of guys never really learn the proper way to shave. In fact, all guys have questions about shaving, whether they've been at it a couple of years already or whether they're watching those pesky chin hairs finally poke through. Regardless of your hair count or experience, I've got answers to your questions:

Q: *How do I know when to start shaving?*

A: Sometime around the age of twelve or thirteen, you'll begin noticing fuzz on your top lip and a few longer, thicker whiskers beginning to sprout from your chin. The amount and timing are different for all guys, but once these start becoming visible, for instance, to a person standing near you, it's time to consider shaving. Try the "pinch test." If you can pinch a whisker between your thumb and forefinger, it's long enough to shave it off. You may be proud of your ability to grow facial hair, but trust me, the peach fuzz thing is no good.

Q: *Electric or blade?*

A: That's up to you. Each option has its advantages and disadvantages. An electric razor can be cleaner, faster, and far more convenient since you can do it dry. Going electric is particularly helpful when you're just getting started. But it doesn't give you as close a shave and may eventually have difficulty mowing down the really tough stubble.

That's why every guy needs to learn to shave with a regular blade. A blade can give you a close, smooth shave, but it takes more time. You can't race through a razor shave unless you want to bloody your face. You'll also need some extras:

shaving cream, a mirror, and
warm water.

There are two kinds of blade
razors: the disposable kind you
can trash after a handful of uses,
and the nicer kind that requires
you to change out blades. Whatever you use, always make sure

BIG TIP:

Tons of guys swear they get
their closest and most
comfortable shave using the
Mach3 razor from Gillette.

your blades are new and sharp. A dull blade will result in what
the industry commonly refers to as "nicks and cuts." Quick tip: I
know tons of guys who swear by the Gillette Mach3. (And no,
they're not paying me to say that.)

Q: *Anything else I should know?*

A: Yep. Your newly smooth skin needs to be protected after
you shave. Take good care of your skin by applying moisturizing
lotion or even warm water to soothe any irritation. Don't use an
alcohol-based product directly after shaving, as it will dry out
your skin and burn like fire on your face. If necessary, don't forget to stop the bleeding.

SMELLING GOOD

You have 2.6 million sweat glands in your body. And that's
a good thing, because sweating is your body's natural way of
regulating heat. When your muscles work overtime, when you
get nervous, or even when you eat spicy food, sweat glands
kick in to cool you down. Fortunately, those millions of sweat
glands themselves don't make you smell. Unfortunately, something else in huge supply on your body does: bacteria. You've
got bacteria all over your skin and hair, particularly in
cramped, warm, moist places like your armpits, your feet, or

around your genitals. When the sweat hits the bacteria—that's when you become a stink zone.

There are several ways for guys to keep body odor to a minimum. The best and most obvious is to shower frequently, once in the morning and, if necessary, again at the end of the day. A little soap and water after you've gotten sweaty does wonders. (Regular soap is fine, but some guys need extra stink-fighting *oomph* and must use a deodorant or antibacterial soap.) Gear up with clean clothes afterward and you'll be just fine.

But most guys can't just jump willy-nilly into the shower at all hours of the day. That's why the good Lord invented deodorants and antiperspirants. Deodorants blast away bacterial odor with pleasant smells that might remind you, for instance, of a mountain stream or a fresh meadow. (These products are helpfully labeled with names like "Mountain Stream" and "Fresh Meadow," by the way.) Antiperspirants, on the other hand, actually reduce the amount of sweat produced by the body wherever they're applied.

Your best choice is probably a deodorant-antiperspirant combo. Find a scent that's right for you in a spray, stick, or roll-on—most guys prefer a clear application so it doesn't show—and put it on each morning after you shower. A light underarm application is usually enough to disguise your smell. Be careful not to overdo it, though, à la Jonathan Capewell.

What about cologne? Cologne works if you play by the rules. Rule one: It isn't designed to cover up an odor. Put it on when you're already stinky and sweaty, and all you'll get is a sickening stew of smells. Rule two: Keep it subtle. Apply too much of it, and you'll have the pleasure of listening to the people around you gag amid your environmentally unsound cologne cloud. Cologne should be used to give your body a signature scent, and it should be used sparingly. If you use a spray, never spray more than two applications. If you prefer a regular cologne bottle, dab a tiny amount—just a drop or two—on your favorite application points: behind your ears, on your neck below your jaw line, or on the inside of your wrists. A little goes a long way. Two or three drops by finger should be all you'll ever need. As an extra bonus, the low-key approach makes expensive colognes last longer.

ZIT CITY

So now your face is smooth, you've figured out how to smell good without accidentally OD'ing, and you're ready to take on the world, right? Wrong. Because suddenly there's a new development. On your face.

A honking bulbous pimple just erupted on your forehead. Uh-oh. What do you do?

> Option A: It's a volcano ready to blow its top. Pop that sucker like a man.
> Option B: Time to break out the old school sweatband across the forehead.
> Option C: Stay home until your face has completely cleared up. Or grow bangs.
> Option D: None of the above. Once you get a zit, the damage is done.

If you answered *Option D*, you win. It's the truth. Once that baby busts out of your skin, the best thing you can do is leave it alone. Here's the sitch: A pimple or zit or blemish or whatever you want to call it is nothing more than a clogged pore. During puberty, your hair follicles produce an oil called *sebum*. This is normal. Sebum, however, tends to trap dirt and bacteria and dead skin cells and all sorts of crap that can end up clogging your pores.

And I think I speak for all of us in saying "Bleh."

Terminology time. When the pore gets completely closed off, a *whitehead* will form. When you get a partially closed pore, it often mixes with the aforementioned dead skin or dirt and you end up with a *blackhead*. When you combine a closed-off pore with bacteria (which, you'll recall, is something our skin has in great supply), the infected, swollen area turns into something called a *papule*. Which sounds a lot cooler than it really is.

FOUR THINGS YOU CAN DO TO CRACK BACK ON ACNE

1. Keep your hands off your face. This means keeping the zit-popping to a minimum. I know it's fun. I know you feel a sense of accomplishment when you finally break the will of a stubborn whitehead and send it packing, but trust me—you're doing more harm than good. Popping a zit is like tearing a hole in your skin. A popped zit can get even more infected. It can scab. It can discolor. It can leave you with a crater. The pinching action can cause it to close off even more. So, cowboy . . . easy on the poppage.

2. Keep your face clean. Wash thoroughly with warm water and a gentle antibacterial cleanser every morning and evening to remove dirt and old dried-up skin cells before they scoot their way into a pore. Hard scrubbing isn't necessary, and will probably do more harm than good because it can irritate acne and cause it to redden. A mild astringent will also do the trick.

3. Apply a benzoyl peroxide product if necessary. This is the over-the-counter stuff you can get at most drugstores or grocery stores to treat mild cases of acne. Apply it to specific problem areas before going to bed and it should help reduce redness, dry out pimples, and generally reduce acne while you sleep. If you have a really bad case of lumpy and/or painful acne, don't rule out a trip to the dermatologist. If Doc thinks you need something a little more powerful than Clearasil, he or she can prescribe it.

4. Just grow up. This isn't exactly good news, but it's true: The best way to get rid of acne is to get older. Honestly, every teenage guy is going to struggle with zit-dom. It's a fact of life. All that sebum production is hormone-related, so until your body slows down on the transition-to-manhood thing, pimples are gonna be an issue. (And sometimes it doesn't even clear up after your teen years. I still struggle with the occasional unwanted blackhead, and nobody's confusing me for a teenager.) Truth is, everybody's going through it, everybody's gonna eventually get over it, and until you do, you might as well relax.

> **THE REAL DEAL:**
>
> The best way to get rid of acne is to get older. You can do stuff to minimize it, but nothing will ultimately destroy it until you grow out of the raging hormone stage.

OUTSIDE VS. INSIDE

One final word before we close up shop on this chapter, courtesy of the Old Testament. I know what you're thinking: *Grooming tips from the Bible?* Not exactly. More like *anti-*grooming tips. It comes from a story in 1 Samuel 16. The prophet Samuel has received word from God that one of Jesse's sons is to be anointed king. So Samuel throws a big sacrificial party in Bethlehem and invites Jesse and the boys. Leaving little David behind to watch the sheep, Jesse brings his finest to the sacrifice and parades them in front of Samuel. They're handsome, noble, broad-shouldered boys. Clear complexions, big muscles, thick beards (the Mach3 wasn't around back then). These guys look like kings. Son #1, Eliab, passes by, and Samuel thinks, *Surely this guy is the one God has chosen!* but—no word from the Lord. So Abinadab does his little song and dance. Still nothing. Shammah steps up to the plate. Nope. Finally, all seven of Jesse's weird-named sons have passed in front of the prophet, but God's been quiet.

Samuel's getting a little concerned at this point, so God offers some explanation: "Do not consider his appearance or his height, for I have rejected him. The LORD does not look at the things man looks at. Man looks at the outward appearance, but the LORD looks at the heart" (1 Samuel 16:7).

Samuel, to his credit, finally gets it. He does a little prodding and finds out Jesse's got one more kid back at the ranch—David, a nobody teenager. Bingo. Guess whom Samuel anointed king? Not the big guys with the muscles and shiny teeth and dimpled chins, but David. The kid was handsome enough, but not so much that his own father gave him any shot at being made king. David probably had a zit or two. His beard was probably scraggly or nonexistent. Most likely he smelled like sheep. But on the inside? On the inside, he was exactly what

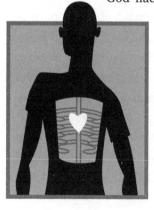

God had in mind. Here was a guy who loved God with all his heart, soul, and strength, and to the Creator of the universe, that was what mattered.

Man looks at the outward stuff, and that's okay. We live in an image-obsessed world and we can deal with that. But God's more interested in the inside stuff. Get that right, and the outside will take care of itself.

CHAPTER 7
DRESS LIKE A MAN

Clothes make the man.

Has anyone ever said that to you? Ever read it before in a book or seen it as a headline in *GQ* or *Maxim*? No? Have you ever seen *any* headlines in *Maxim*? Or are you always too distracted by the pics of celebrity babes in their underwear?

Yeah. Me, too.

But let's focus. "Clothes make the man" is a statement you'll hear every now and then in our society. It goes way back. As far as I can tell, the first person to ever say it was a Roman orator—a guy who gave speeches for a living—named Quintilian. He lived in the first century, around the same time as Jesus. So the idea has been around longer than you'd think. Certainly a lot longer than any clothing styles you'd be interested in. Toga, anyone?

But back to that statement itself. What does "clothes make the man" mean? There are a couple of ways to define it. First, it means that how a man dresses will establish his status—it helps people identify him. Second, that the way a guy looks on the outside can influence how he feels on the inside. Let's take a closer look at these two meanings.

What do you think when you see a guy wearing the following outfits?

> A big Stetson hat, cowboy boots, and dusty, boot-cut Wranglers

> Khakis, penny loafers, and a tucked-in dress shirt

> Ghetto-sagged jeans, a throwback NBA jersey, and old-school Adidas

> A crisp black suit, slacks, and tie

> Ripped, faded jeans and an old Screaming Trees tee

What conclusions jump out at you? Anything? Do you make a snap decision about a guy based on his "uniform"? If not, then you're different from everyone else in the world, because we're all guilty of judging people by their appearance—and clothes play a major role in the way we look. If we see somebody decked out as a cowboy, we probably think—right or wrong—that he's a simple, rural guy. Not too bright, not too sophisticated, probably sports a barnyard aroma. We see a guy kicking it in FUBU or Rocawear and immediately decide he's into urban culture and hip-hop. Or worse, we think he might be a thug. And any guy still wearing a suit and tie these days must be either a lawyer or a banker or a mortician, because they're the only ones dressing up these days, right?

Here's something to chew on: When you meet someone new, you tend to make up your mind about them in less than thirty seconds. The impression you give during that first half-minute is crucial, and a major part of it, for better or worse, has to do with what you're wearing. Our

> **THE REAL DEAL:**
>
> People will decide whether they like you or not within thirty seconds of meeting you, and a major part of that first impression comes from your clothing.

society stereotypes people based on the way they look. It's not fair, but these days, what you wear indicates who you are.

There's another aspect of "clothes make the man" that deals with your emotional state. It's the idea that how you dress on the outside has a lot to do with how you feel on the inside. Here's how it works. Have you ever had to wear a tux for a wedding or a formal dance? Did it make you feel more sophisticated or grown up? (Or, at the least, more uncomfortable?) What about your lounging-around-the-house gear? Does putting on your most comfy, frayed jeans and your favorite T-shirt actually help you relax after a long day at school? It does for me. Changing clothes after work helps me wind down.

What about athletic uniforms? Any guy who has ever played team sports knows that he feels different once he puts on his uni. There's something about squeezing into your shoulder pads or strapping on your shin guards that cranks your energy level. You get pumped by the adrenaline rush and anticipation. Guys become more aggressive and intense when they gear up for a game, and clothing is the catalyst.

That's why the way you dress is important. Not only can it determine what other people think about you, but it plays a role in the way you actually feel about yourself. Toga Dude was right: Clothes make the man.

WHAT ARE YOUR CLOTHES SAYING?

Keep in mind that your clothes are *only* a symbol, and sometimes people get the symbolism wrong. Fair or not, people will stereotype you based on how you dress. You may be as strait-laced as they come, but wear ratty jeans and a wrinkled T-shirt, and people—especially adults—will tag you as a slob. On the other hand, you may actually *be* a world-class slacker, but wear crisp khakis and a button-down, and your teachers may just treat you with more respect. Fair? Nope. But true. All I'm saying is, keep it in mind. Be yourself. Dress with creativity and your own style, but be aware of the consequences.

DISCLAIMER TIME

Now, after all this time telling you that "clothes make the man"—for better or for worse—I'm gonna take it back. Just a little.

Why? Because some guys put way too much stock in how they dress. We make fun of girls for doing the same thing, but guys can be just as bad. I know because I was one of them. I thought I could mesh better with the "in" crowd by wearing more expensive jeans. I thought my little dip into the world of fashion would change my life.

Didn't work for me. Won't work for you.

Besides, what if it *had* worked? What if I'd gotten a whole new set of friends simply because I wore the right pair of stupid jeans? Talk about shallow. Talk about materialistic. Why would I even *want* friends like that?

Clothes may make the man, but only for an instant. You might get a feeling of sophistication from your tuxedo or a jolt of adren-

aline while gearing up for
football, but that inner
change is fleeting. It doesn't
last. And to be honest, any
guy can dress however he
wants on the outside, and it
won't really change who he is

> **THE REAL DEAL:**
>
> Clothes may make the man, but
> the makeover only lasts for an
> instant.

on the inside. Fashion comes and goes and comes and goes again.
But who you really are deep down inside doesn't change when you
put on a new shirt or lace up new shoes. What you look like on the
outside is only part of what God is doing with you on the inside.

The way you dress won't change your life. But I'd be lying if I
told you it wasn't important. It is.

And for that reason, it's time to step away from all the philoso-
phy stuff. Let's tackle something more practical. You need real
advice, right? Following is a hodgepodge list of some of the essentials of manly fashion.

BOXERS VS. BRIEFS

Let's start at the bottom. Literally. The great
debate among men of all ages is what to wear
down there. Where you stand—er, sit—on the
issue is more than a matter of personal prefer-
ence. It's a window into your personality. Back

when I was a teenager, I remember a big fuss being made over a

question asked of then–presidential candidate
Bill Clinton during a 1992 interview on MTV.
The question: *Do you wear boxers or briefs?*
For the record, Clinton answered that he

was a briefs guy. No word on whether that answer earned the young questioner's vote. But back then, it was no contest. Whitey-tighties were the top-selling underwear. In recent years, though, boxer love has been growing. Research indicates guys in their teens and twenties definitely prefer boxers to briefs. Maybe you've already made your choice.

Keep in mind, though, that one style is no more or less manly than another. Boxers may look a little better, but let's be honest— who's gonna see your underwear besides the guys in the locker room? It's really just a matter of which you prefer. To complicate the issue, the trendy boxer-brief combo is becoming more and more popular, and soon may bridge the gap between the two camps. Until then, the decision is yours.

BE FINICKY ABOUT FIT

Guys have been subject to an unfortunate trend over the last several years, to our detriment. I've given in to the trend, you've given in to the trend, and to be truthful, we've all looked pretty silly being such slaves to idiotic fashion. What trend am I bashing? I'll gloss it with the simplest name I can think of, for lack of a more creative description: Clothes That Don't Fit. The biggest fashion mistake guys make is buying clothes that are too big—or too small—for our bodies.

Things are changing, though. For the past few years, baggy pants and shirts have been the norm for teenage guys, and honestly, we've all begun to look like we just lost fifty pounds on a diet but are still wearing our old clothes. And even though we're trying so hard to style, it's tough to look good in clown pants. You have to keep hiking them up to prevent a peep show. You end up with frayed and grimy hems because they're dragging beneath your heels as you walk. Baggy clothes look sloppy and give the impression that you could care less how you come off. And guess what? They're no longer off the hizzle.

BIG TIP:

The biggest fashion mistake most guys make is wearing clothes that don't fit. These days, baggy and oversized is out. The clean, neat look is in.

Baggy is out.

These days, guys are going for a cleaner style, and the fitted, neat look is in. Whether you're wearing jeans, cargoes, plain-front khakis, or whatever, make sure they fit.

And one more thing, while we're on the subject: Stuff that fits too tight is also a no-no. You may have a rockin' six-pack, but that still doesn't mean you can pull off a skintight wife-beater or tank. It may make you look more cut, but it's way tacky. If you absolutely have to show off your abs, join the swim team.

HOW TO TIE A TIE

The Onassis. The Shelby. The Diagonal. The Four-in-Hand, Double Windsor, and Half-Windsor. If it sounds to you like I've just listed the names of a bunch of professional wrestling moves, then you need a quick lesson in ties. The weird names above are different kinds of knots men use to tie a necktie. Some are more fashionable than others. Some are more difficult. But, as a guy, you need to know how to tie at least one of these knots.

Why? Because at some point in your life, you're going to need to put on a real tie and have it look right. (Clip-ons don't count, Maynard.) It might be for a job interview once you're out of college.

It might be for a wedding or a funeral. Maybe there's a semiformal dance coming up. Whatever the case, you can't rely on Mom or Dad to hook you up with a tie forever, so pay attention as we speed through a quick tutorial, complete with handy illustrations.

We'll tackle the Four-in-Hand. It's probably the simplest and most popular knot to tie, and the end result is narrow and neat. Here's your step-by-step:

1. Find a mirror. Like shaving, tying a tie is much easier if you're looking in a mirror. Also, find a tie.

2. Drape the tie around the back of your neck, beneath your collar. Start with the fat end hanging at least a foot below the skinny end (figure A). It doesn't matter which side (right or left) the fat end hangs on. Just go with whatever feels most comfortable to you.

3. Wrap Fatty over and then back behind Skinny (figure B).

4. Bring Fatty back around and in front of Skinny yet again. The fat end has now completely encircled the skinny end (figure C).

5. Pull Fatty up through the loop between your collar and the tie (figure D).

6. Hold on to the front of the knot with your index finger to keep some slack in it, then bring the fat end down through the main loop you just made with Steps 2 and 3 (figure E).

7. Pull the fat end down until the knot is snug. Then, holding the skinny end, carefully slide the knot up toward your collar. If, at this point, you begin to choke and gasp for air, you've pulled it too tight (figure F). Duh.

8. Sometimes you'll finish up a tie and discover that, unfortunately, the narrow end is hanging below the fat end. That's just plain wrong. So you'll have two choices. Choice A: Start over with the fat end and hang it lower than you did the first time. Or Choice B: Just leave it like it is and endure the mockery of your friends with perfect ties. If the fat end hangs down too low, decrease the difference in lengths at the beginning, and start over. And don't get frustrated: You need the practice, rookie.

9. Once it's perfect, smile at yourself in the mirror. Handsome devil.

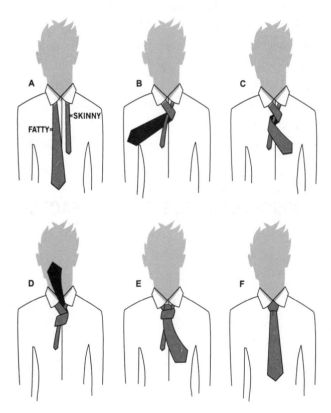

STEP TO MANHOOD #99

Learning to tie your own tie.

Bonus Tip: So you've successfully put on your tie, you go to your tie-requiring function, and by the time you get home you're ready to rip that thing from your neck and give yourself some breathing room. Am I right? Pay attention: Half the guys in the universe screw this next part up, because the punks never learned how to do it correctly. There is a right and a wrong way to remove or untie a necktie. The thing you should *not* do is slide the knot down so you can yank the whole contraption up and over your head. Nor should you pull the fat end back through the narrow knot, as this can crush your tie and twist up its guts. Instead, just repeat the tie-tying steps above in reverse order. This keeps your ties—which can be expensive, mind you—from becoming distorted.

MISCELLANEOUS FASHION FACTS

BELTS

Most guys need to own three belts: a black dress belt, a brown dress belt, and a casual belt. The general rule is to make sure your dress belt and shoes always match. So put on the black belt when you bust out the black ECCOs, the brown belt when you slip on the brown Docs, and the casual belt when you go with the sneaks.

SOCKS

Every guy's wardrobe ought to have a few pairs of dress socks, since white athletic tube socks aren't appropriate for everything. Socks ought to match (or be slightly darker than) your pants, so every guy needs to have at least a pair or two of black dress socks, navy dress socks, and non-white casual socks (the thicker style of socks with different patterns or textures).

APPEARANCE

Scientists who study human behavior have come up with a list of the first things we notice about a person upon meeting them. In order, we notice skin color, age, sex, bearing (height/weight) and, finally, appearance. Here's something to think about: Appearance is last on that list, but it's the only characteristic you have control over. You can't do anything about your age. Changing your sex is not something I'd really recommend. And unless you're a self-tanning freak, adjusting your skin color is pretty much out. But your outside appearance? That's yours, baby. Ball's in your court. Even though we'd all be perfectly content to wear ratty jeans and T-shirts the rest of our lives, we need to look at ourselves from an outside standpoint. Always ask: *What impression am I giving by the way I dress?* Then, whenever possible, take care to make sure your clothing presents a positive, accurate first impression.

Remember, guys, the most important rule of fashion is to be yourself. While it's important to be considerate of others in how you dress, it's equally important to keep it real. That means dressing according to your personality. It also means not being a mindless follower of trends. Just because some ripped, stubble-faced Hollywood "It" boy has begun wearing leprechaun-green socks with all of his outfits does *not* mean you need to do the same. Never wear something only because it's stylish. Wear it because it makes you look good *and* feel good.

CHAPTER 8
HEALTH AND EXERCISE

Three reasons guys are working out. There are plenty of reasons people work out these days. First, it's healthy. In the U.S. and around the world, obesity—which is a medical term that means weighing at least 30 percent more than your ideal body weight—is becoming more and more of a problem. Experts say one in five teens are overweight. There are lots of reasons for this, but one of the big ones is that we do a lot more sitting around than we used to. We spend hours each day on the computer, watching TV, or playing video games. It's good for the hand-eye coordination, but not so good for the heart and lungs and muscles. Combine that inactivity with our love for tacos and burgers and chili fries, and we've got a whole nation of fast-food addicts and unhealthy teenagers. Being overweight as a teen can have some pretty nasty health consequences as you get older, like heart disease and diabetes. That's why physical activity—strength training, jogging, competitive sports—is almost always a good idea for guys.

Reason number two people are working out: It gives them a competitive edge. Even though the idea of lifting weights with my scrawny little arms seemed

> **THE REAL DEAL:**
>
> One in five teens are overweight, and part of the problem is that we load up on fast food and slack off on exercise.

about as fun to me as, for instance, getting my tongue tattooed, my coach was right. You want to be a better athlete, you gotta work out. Now, there are a lot of things that factor into your ability to excel in the athletic world. Much of it is God-given talent. Some soccer players have especially quick feet. Some track stars are just born fast. That's due to heredity and genetics, and there's not much you can do about those. But the best athletes are the ones who work hard, on and off the court. A dedicated training regimen goes a long way toward making you a better performer, and that's a major reason teenage guys start weight training.

Reason number three for working out: It makes you look good for the ladies. Time for some smack-upside-the-head honesty, guys. Girls like a fit, lean, and strong man. Back in the day, girls wanted a guy with a strong chin and broad shoulders. Today they're looking for ripped triceps, pectoral definition, and a nice, sculpted six-pack down the middle. Some psychiatrists believe that out of all the guys who work out, as many are in it to look good as are interested in getting stronger. Weight training is like lipstick and eyeliner for guys. It's a way to improve our appearance.

WEIGHT-TRAINING HOW-TOS

Regardless of the whys, you're probably interested in how to do it, right? Well, I'm no Mr. Universe (as the above story just made painfully clear), but I can give you the following tips:

ABS

Mags like *Men's Health* regularly list the abs as the "most desirable part of the body," according to women. Therefore, guys are usually more interested in achieving rock-hard abs than anything else. So I've got good and bad news for you. The good: It's really not that difficult to strengthen the abdominal muscles. In fact, you can do it without the expense of a gym membership or weight-training equipment. The bad: The key to shapely abs has a whole lot more to do with diet than it does exercise.

Here's why. Most guys' abs are hidden under a layer of body fat. And as long as that layer of fat is there, you're not going to be able to see your abs. Only guys with body fat below 10 percent will have visible abs. Got that? It doesn't matter how many crunches you do, you're wasting your time if you're trying to get a six-pack without reducing your body fat. How do you reduce the fat? By eating right and burning calories via aerobic exercise (for more on aerobic exercise, keep reading below). So cut down on the greasy food and get moving. Go with carrots instead of cookies. Lesson over.

That said, the absolute best way to strengthen the upper abdominals is through that old P.E. class standby: crunches. Lie on your back and bend your legs, putting your knees up in the air so your thighs are at a right angle to your torso. Raise your shoulders off the ground while curling your breastbone toward your hips. Ease back down. Repeat slowly until you can feel the burn.

A good way to work the lower ab muscles is with lower leg raises. Lie down with your legs flat against the floor. Raise both legs a few inches off the ground and try to hold them there for at least thirty seconds, using only your abs to provide the tension. Once you've counted to thirty, *slowly* lower your legs back down. Sound easy? It's not. Do five or six of these in repetition.

ARMS

Visit a gym, and it's likely that two-thirds of the guys you see there are working on their arms. Everyone wants shapely triceps and bulging biceps. Good thing there are about twenty thousand different ways to achieve twenty-inch guns, but how do you know which technique is the best? You don't. There are lots of ways to do it, and most of them work, provided you have the desire and dedication.

One hit method of pumping up the biceps is a curling workout called "21s." This breaks the basic curling motion into three sections. Start with a smaller amount of weight—maybe half of your max. Perform a regular curl, but instead of pulling the weight all the way up, stop in the middle at 90 degrees. You'll end with your arms bent at the elbows, forming an *L*. Do that seven times. Your next set of reps will begin at the middle "L" position, and you will be bringing the barbell all the way up to your chest at the top. Do that another seven times. Your final set of reps will be the standard curl, 180 degrees from bottom to top. It's basic math—combine three sets of seven reps and you get twenty-one.

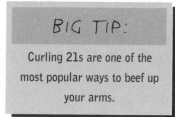

BIG TIP:

Curling 21s are one of the most popular ways to beef up your arms.

For the triceps, a good exercise is the close-grip bench press, which is similar to a basic bench press (see description in the "chest" section) except your hands are positioned less than six inches apart on the bar—close enough for your thumbs to touch each other. Another option is the triceps dip, which is like doing push-ups for your triceps. Start by sitting in a chair, supporting yourself with your hands at the sides of your hips. Pull your butt down in front of the chair until your elbows near 90 degrees, then push yourself back up. Do this one carefully, though, and make sure you keep your shoulders level.

CHEST

My nemesis, the bench press, is still one of the best ways to pump up your pectoral muscles—the muscles in your chest. Lie on your back on the bench, making sure your abs are tight and your lower back is flat. Start with the weight bar directly over your chest. Grab it with your elbows at 90-degree angles, and push your arms straight up. Just before you get to a locked position, lower the bar back to where you started. Use a weight that allows you to do at least two sets of twelve to fifteen reps, and build up from there. (Hopefully you'll be able to handle more than just the bar.)

If you don't have a set of weights handy, then push-ups are the way to go for building up the pecs. I'm going to assume you know what a push-up is. Just remember to lower your body until your elbows are at 90-degree angles before pushing back up. And don't droop in the middle—keep your abs tight throughout.

LAST TIP

If you're going to begin working out with free weights, take advantage of the opportunity and start your strength training with a friend. It's generally a good idea to have a spotter in place any time you're lifting, even if you're using smaller weights, and even if you know what you're doing. Even if you're huge. Why? Because there's no guarantee you'll be able to bench that final rep. Find someone to hang with you while you work out, someone who's also interested in getting fit or who has a little more experience. A spotter will encourage you, make sure you perform each exercise correctly, and be there to bail should you need him. Trust me: Working out is a lot more fun—and a lot safer—when you're with a friend.

BIG TIP:

Workouts are safer and more fun if you tag-team it with a friend.

ONE MORE MUSCLE
YOU SHOULDN'T FORGET

Is weight training the only way to get into shape? No way. It's just half of the picture. There's a lot more to exercising than pumping iron. Weight training is a good way to burn calories and strengthen bones and muscles, but you also need to find a way to beef up another muscle, the most important and strongest one you have: your heart. The heart is a muscle, and like any other muscle, it needs a good workout now and then. In fact, most experts recommend that you give your heart a good workout at least three times a week at twenty minutes a pop, in order to stay healthy and prevent future problems. How do you pump up the heart? By doing something called *aerobic exercise.*

To put it very simply—without getting into all the science stuff—aerobic exercise is any kind of exertion that gets your heart pumping and requires your lungs to work harder to deliver oxygen to your body. Jogging is an aerobic exercise. So is swimming. Basketball, soccer, competitive volleyball, biking, gymnastics, martial arts, and even brisk walking are considered aerobic exercise. That means you don't have to belong to some fancy fitness club or aerobics class to pump up your heart. All you have to do is move around a little.

STEP TO MANHOOD #16

Dedicate yourself to a well-rounded fitness regimen that combines strength training with aerobic training for optimum health.

Remember, the best path to fitness is to combine strength training with aerobic training. Get strong and look good by working out individual muscle groups like your abs and biceps. Stay healthy by working out the heart and lungs.

THE FINAL SECRET
TO STAYING IN SHAPE

We've focused a lot on strength training in this chapter, simply because that's what a lot of guys are into these days. But, again, that doesn't mean pumping iron is the only way to get fit. There are lots of ways to exercise. Team sports are always a fun way to stay in shape, whether it's with your school or a club. Solo exercise is also cool—some guys like the solitude of an early morning jog before school. Other guys are into bicycling or martial arts. It doesn't matter what you do, as long as you get off your butt a few times each week.

Wanna know a secret? You don't even have to do "official" exercise to actually exercise. I define exercise as *a refusal to be lazy*. You know how Mom or Dad make a big deal out of getting the good parking spot near the front of the mall? That's lazy. Instead, ask them to park as far away as possible. They probably need the walk as much as you do. While you're at the mall, use the stairs instead of the escalator or elevator. Turn off the TV and chase your little cousins or nieces and nephews around the house. Help out with the vacuuming once in a while. Walk the dog. Mow the yard. Believe it or not, all of these things can be considered exercise because they get your heart pumping and burn calories. They're the opposite of laziness. They get you away from all the screen time (television, computers, video games) that threatens to make ordinarily healthy guys like yourself into lazy slugs.

God didn't intend for you to be a lazy slug. Get moving. Be strong. Have fun. Be fit.

CHAPTER 9

THE SEX CHAPTER

Let me guess. You opened this book, found the table of contents, breezed through the list, saw a chapter called "The Sex Chapter," and—*wham!*—here you are.

Right?

How did I know that's what you'd do? Because I'm a guy. And when I was your age, that's exactly what I would have done. A whole chapter about sex? I'm there.

Guys of all ages—and teenage guys in particular—are very interested in sex. And I mean VERY. Sure, we get into stuff like sports or skateboarding or gaming or even church, but the one thing that trips through our brains all the time, the one thing we're more curious about than anything else, is sex. Physically and chemically, guys are wired for sex. It's absolutely normal. It's the way God made us. It has a purpose. And it's—let's be honest—a whole lot of fun.

But it can also be very confusing. I grew up in a loving, close Christian family. We all got along great, had fun together, went camping and fishing a lot, spent a lot of time with one another. But my family didn't talk very much about personal stuff. That wasn't really my personality; it wasn't really my parents' personalities, either. So needless to say, there was very little discussion about sex at my house when I was growing up. In fact, to my knowledge, there was only *one* sex talk that involved me. Just one.

91

It happened one afternoon when we were driving to New Mexico for a skiing weekend. It was just us guys, and my little brother was asleep in the backseat. Dad was driving. He reached under the seat and pulled out a book called *Almost Twelve.*

"I wanted to give you this book," Dad said. "It's about sex."

My ears pricked up. I'd never heard Dad say the word *sex* before. I was interested. And uncomfortable. Sex wasn't something I wanted to talk about with my dad.

"It talks about some things you need to know," he said, "but you probably know all this stuff already. Maybe from the guys or something."

I believe my response was, "Unhngh."

"Anyway, I thought you might want to read it, and if you have any questions you can ask me. Okay?"

Me, staring out the window: "Okay." He handed me the book.

That, friends, was the first and only time I discussed sex with either of my parents. And, to be honest, the lack of conversation didn't exactly break my heart. I was interested in the topic, but not so interested in discussing it with Dad. Don't get me wrong—my dad was a great dad. I loved him back then and I love him now. But neither of us was cut out for the sex talk, and I'm guessing a lot of you feel the same way about your family. Family sex talks can involve a whole lot of weirdness, and for good reason. Most guys aren't going to come home from school some afternoon and say, "Hey there, Mom and Dad. I've got some questions about sex. Might we sit down after dinner and discuss masturbation?"

Not in a million years.

So, back to the book Dad gave me. It was basically a birds-and-the-bees kind of thing: Guys have a penis, girls have a vagina; sperm and eggs and ovulation and intercourse. All the basics of the baby-making process. It was informative, I guess, but it was almost like biology for twelve-year-olds. I didn't want a science lecture. I wanted some specific answers to some specific personal questions. *Embarrassing* questions. And that book didn't provide the answers.

And if I didn't feel comfortable talking about that stuff with Mom or Dad, I *sure* didn't want to ask my friends any of the questions I had. Why? Because my friends acted like they had all the answers already! I'd look like a total loser if I admitted that a lot of that stuff was unclear to me. They were talking about making out and boners and "getting to third base" and I figured they knew what they were talking about, even if I had no idea what "third base" involved. But you know what? They were just as confused as I was. We were all clueless together, but none of us wanted to admit it.

Here's something you need to know: It's true that a lot of kids are experimenting with sex at earlier and earlier ages. In fact, some of your classmates have probably engaged in sexual activity before, whether it was regular sexual intercourse or oral sex or some form of genital contact. But it's also true that most guys your age don't have all the details. They might think they know it all, and they'll probably *talk* like they know it all, but trust me: *They don't know it all.* They wigged just as much as you did when their parents brought it up. And like you, they're unwilling to bring any of those questions out in the open because it might embarrass them, or it might make them look inexperienced, or it might make them seem like a perv.

> **THE REAL DEAL:**
>
> Your friends may talk a good game and use terminology you don't understand, but they're probably as uninformed about sex as you are.

I know because I went through the exact same thing as a teenager. And because of that, I'm going to try to answer your questions as honestly and accurately as I can. I promise to be up front about it, too. I know what guys talk about in the locker room. I know what guys fantasize about. And I'm not afraid to say "penis." In fact, I may use some terms that aren't considered polite for mixed company. But we're all guys here, so get your snickering out of the way now, and let's get into it.

Eventually, we'll get into an actual question-and-answer session. But first, I want to show you what the Bible says about sex. You might be surprised.

THE STUFF YOU NEVER TALK ABOUT IN SUNDAY SCHOOL

Sex talk doesn't get a lot of play in church, for obvious reasons. In fact, about the only time you hear it mentioned on Sunday mornings or in youth group is when the subject of abstinence comes up. *Abstinence* is just a long word that means "not having sex." And I want to be very clear about this from the start: Not having sex is the way to go for a teenager, especially one who wants to honor God with his body. The Bible's pretty clear that God intended sex to be something shared between a husband and a wife. But when the topic of sex comes up at church the discussion is usually pretty quick: *Should you have sex? No. Wait until you're married.*

Discussion over.

As a result, Christians—guys and girls— can have a hard time talking about sex, because it can almost feel un-Christian to have the kind of specific questions you have. It's almost like sex is off-limits until you're married, *so you better just stop thinking about it right now, young man.*

You and I both know that's impossible, so let me ease your mind. Sex is good, not dirty. Thinking about sex is normal, not dirty. *Wanting* to have sex is normal, not dirty. Sex is something you were specifically designed for. There are graphic sex scenes in the Bible.

Wha—?

It's true. If you were to make a movie of the entire Bible, there are a few parts that would earn it an NC-17 rating due to the sex and nudity and "adult themes." As a teenager, you wouldn't even be allowed in the theater. Weird, huh? After all, you're *supposed* to read your Bible, right?

Check out this passage from Song of Songs, which has scandalized uptight Christians for centuries: "Your stature is like that of the palm, and your breasts like clusters of fruit. I said, 'I will climb the palm tree; I will take hold of its fruit'" (vv. 7–8). That "clusters of fruit" thing is another metaphor, but I think you get the picture.

Here's the point: Parts of the Bible can be very sexy. We just don't like to talk about them, because the topic of sex makes a lot of Christians uncomfortable. We forget that God created sex, and that, once married, we're encouraged to have it as often as we want.

> **BIG TIP:**
>
> The next time your Sunday School teacher asks you what your favorite Bible verse is, tell him it's Ezekiel 23:20. Watch the look on his face when he looks it up and reads it. Then prepare to get into trouble.

QUESTIONS AND ANSWERS

You ask the questions, I'll try to give the answers. Let's go:

Q: *Let's start with the basics. What is sex?*

A: Officially, sex is God's way of making sure humans stick around. It's how we procreate, which is a fancy way of saying "have kids." When guys are sexually aroused, their penises become erect. This makes it easy for the penis to slide into a woman's vagina, an act we call *sexual intercourse.* By this time, both the guy and girl are starting to feel pretty stinkin' good, and eventually the guy will climax—reach orgasm—and ejaculate. (Sometimes the woman will climax, too, but not always.) Upon ejaculation, semen shoots out of the penis, and the millions of reproductive sperm in the semen flow into the vagina, hoping to hook up with the woman's egg. If everything goes right, a baby is created. On a purely practical basis, sex is the process that keeps the human race from dying out.

Q: *But there's more to sex than just making babies, right?*

A: Oh, yeah. God loves us and wants us to enjoy the world he's created, and for that reason, he made sex a heck of a lot of fun. I won't lie to you—sex is good. It feels good when you think about it, it feels good when you start to become aroused while "fooling around" beforehand, and it feels *really* good when you're actually doing it. God made sex intensely pleasurable, and that's why it's such a huge deal in our society.

Q: *Sometimes it seems like my penis has a mind of its own, and an erection shows up out of nowhere.*

A: That's more of a statement than a question. Didn't you read the rules?

Q: *Fine, Mr. Know-It-All. What's with all the trips to Schwiiing City?*

A: A lady on TV once said to a guy about his penis, "I don't know how you guys walk around with those things." She has a good point. Once you hit puberty, the penis starts acting like an unruly stepchild, and you start getting erections a lot more often than you used to. You can get one when you're kissing a girl or when you're *thinking* about kissing a girl. You can get one when you see something sexy on TV or when you read something sexy in a book or magazine. Looking at a picture of a naked or barely dressed woman may give you an erection. Even sitting or lying in a weird position can give you one. Erections usually go away after a few minutes, but there's not much you can do to get rid of them. Theoretically, this shouldn't be much a problem. Unless you're standing up in front of a bunch of people and you're wearing sweatpants, it's doubtful anyone will notice.

Q: *What is a wet dream?*

A: The official name for a wet dream is *nocturnal emission*, and it refers to ejaculation during sleep. When it happens—and, trust me, it will happen—you probably won't realize what's going on until right at the end, during the orgasm. At that point, it's too late—you're stuck with a sticky mess on your underwear or pajamas or sometimes even the bedsheets.

A wet dream is nature's way of relieving tension caused by excess semen buildup—kind of like a water balloon that keeps filling up until it pops. If you haven't had sex or masturbated for several days, your body will release the semen via a wet dream. It may be messy and a little embarrassing (especially if you stain your sheets), but it's perfectly natural. Your parents know guys go through this—even if you haven't talked about it with them—so don't feel like you have to secretly wash your bedding after it happens.

Though wet dreams can occur whether you're actually dreaming or not, they sometimes happen when you're dreaming about having sex (with the orgasm happening at the, ahem, critical point in the dream). Occasionally your "dream lover" may be someone you wouldn't expect, and for this reason, a lot of guys freak about the content of these kinds of dreams. Well, don't. Dreams are weird. They're not something you can control, they're not sinful, and they don't mean anything. They're just dreams. Don't worry about them.

STEP TO MANHOOD #46

Freaking out after your first wet dream because you're certain Mom's gonna see the semen stain next time she does the laundry.

Q: *What about masturbation? Guys at school talk like it's no big deal, but I've heard that Christians shouldn't do it.*

A: Hoo boy. You probably won't ever hear much discussion about it at church or in your youth group, but masturbation is a huge issue for guys—and there's a lot of disagreement among Christians about whether or not it's okay for a guy to masturbate.

Let's cover the essentials first. Masturbation is the act of manually bringing yourself to orgasm and ejaculation by rubbing on the penis. You'll hear it described by a number of different terms. Whatever you call it, it's something a lot of guys do on a regular basis, in private.

Physically, there's nothing wrong with masturbating. You may have heard some myths about it—that it gives you acne or hairy palms, that it makes you go blind, or that it makes you run out of semen—but none of those are true. On the other hand, there's also nothing wrong with *not* masturbating. You don't have to do it if you don't want to.

There's a saying I once heard: Ninety-five percent of men masturbate, and the other 5 percent are lying. And honestly, research backs this up. Studies have shown that nine out of ten people—men *and* women—have done it at least once by the time they've turned twenty-one. Everybody does it, but society has disapproved of it for so long that no one really talks about it.

So what about Christians? Well, the Bible doesn't mention masturbation at all. What the Bible is pretty clear about, though, is that it's wrong to lust. In Matthew 5:28, Jesus equates lustful thoughts with adultery, saying, "Anyone who looks at a woman lustfully has already committed adultery with her in his heart." And for many guys, lustful looking or thinking plays a big role in masturbation. Some guys get off by looking at porn or suggestive photos. Other guys picture themselves in sexual situations. They think about having sex with a real person—either someone they know or an actress or supermodel they idealize. Other times, they may picture some anonymous, imagined fantasy girl. Or maybe they think about having sex with their future wife. This is where it gets tricky. I'm pretty sure it's lustful, according to Jesus' definition, to imagine having sex with someone specific like a hot cheerleader at your school. But what about someone nonspecific? What about someone you've dreamed up in your own mind, like the ideal version of your future wife? What if you're just trying to visualize one of those scenes from Song of Songs?

I told you I'd speak honestly to you about this kind of stuff, and honestly, I'm not prepared to come right out and tell you that masturbation is wrong, or that it's always a sin. Why? Because for every guy, some degree of sexual thought is natural—it's a result of our God-given sex drive. And as a result, I don't believe *every* sexual thought is necessarily lustful of sinful. But *some* are. Taking it to extremes (e.g., masturbating to the collection of porn you hide under your mattress)*is* a sin. No question.

It's worth mentioning that you can masturbate without thinking about sex. In fact, you can even ejaculate while doing something physically intense but nonsexual—I know guys who have while lifting weights or doing crunches.

Sometimes we forget that ejaculation, at the most basic level, is a bodily function. But we should also remember that masturbation is a sexual activity, too. And when combined with lust, it can be sinful. But when it doesn't involve lust? I hesitate to condemn it, particularly because I know every guy is going to struggle with it at some point or another. And we struggle with enough things already—I think there are bigger problems than something guys do alone and in private. So I'm not gonna pile a load of guilt on you for doing it once in a while. It may not be the most popular opinion among Christians, but it's what I think.

Finally, you need to realize that masturbation probably wasn't what God had in mind when he created your sex drive. Your penis was made to fit nicely into the vagina of your future wife. It wasn't designed to fit nicely into your sweaty palm. Masturbation is a kind of sex, but it's certainly not the best kind.

Q: *What about pornography?*

A: That's an easy one. There's nothing positive about porn. *Nothing.* Thanks to the Internet and e-mail spam, it's easier now than ever before for guys to look at naked women. When I was a teenager you had to score a mag like *Playboy.* These days, all you have to do is get on a spammer's contact list and you'll have more sexual images than you can handle delivered directly to your in-box.

Guys look at porn because we're curious. We're interested in anything sex-related, including what the different parts of the female body look like. I've heard the teenage years described as a "daily search for nudity." Guys get turned on visually, and boobs and butts and the stuff in between really push our buttons. Is it a sin to see a naked female body? No. There are nude females in classic paintings, and illustrations in the textbook for your health class. These aren't considered pornography, and I doubt they cause you to lust.

But there are several big problems with porn. One is that porn is *designed* to cause lust. That's its purpose. Jesus was pretty clear when he said looking at a woman lustfully was as sinful as adultery. I dare you to tell me that when you look at a naked centerfold or some big-breasted blonde on a porn site, you're not automatically thinking what it would be like to do something sexual with her.

Another problem is that it can fill your mind with unrealistic ideas and expectations about women. The women who pose for pornography look perfect, because their flaws have been digitally hidden with fancy programs like Photoshop. They're usually tan (even in bikini zones) and have paid gobs of money (i.e., plastic surgery) to look so good. If you get married in the future, it will probably not be to someone who looks like

THE REAL DEAL:

Hardly any women actually look like the women who pose for porn. Real breasts don't look like that without plastic surgery, and women never pose like that. To think they do is sexist and demeaning.

that. A lifetime of drooling over porn stars will give you the wrong idea about how a woman's body should look. And trust me, the last thing your wife or girlfriend wants is for you to compare her body with that of a porn star. Real boobs don't look like that without plastic surgery, and women *never* pose like that. To think they do is sexist and the result of too much nudie time.

Pornography is demeaning, too. Not just for the women who choose to pose for it, but for all women everywhere who hate the idea that the porn industry is encouraging females to be viewed only as sex objects—as nothing more than images for guys to lust over. Think about this: How would your mom feel if she knew you were viewing pornography? What if your little sister discovered pictures you'd downloaded? That kind of thing happens a lot. Unless you're a computer whiz, it's hard to hide your browsing habits.

The worst part of porn is that it's just as addictive as drugs or alcohol. Once you experience that sweaty-palmed feeling as you sit at your computer waiting for BigBosomedBeauties.com to load, it's hard to find something else to replace that sexual adrenaline rush. I know of guys who used to spend every moment they had looking for free porn sites. Porn addiction is a real problem, even for Christians—heck, even for a lot of *pastors*. If it's something you struggle with, don't feel like you're a freak. You're not. You're just an average, normal guy who's let his curiosity spin out of control. Find an adult you can trust and spill your guts. Ask him for help. If he's a guy, he'll understand.

Q: *How far can I go with my girlfriend and still remain a virgin?*

A: That's the question guys have been asking for years, particularly since the whole President Clinton and Monica

Lewinsky scandal. Here's what the question really means: *I know if you have sexual intercourse then you've lost your virginity, and I don't think I want to do that yet. But am I still a virgin if I've had oral sex?*

Technically, yes. But where do you get the idea God is into technicalities? Jesus spent a lot of time in the Bible condemning the Pharisees, who meticulously followed the rules but forgot that God's more interested in the heart. Oral sex may keep you within the rules of virginity, but can you honestly justify that you're not having sex? If it's not sex, then what is it? I'll tell you what it is—it's a way to have sex without officially having sex. And if I know and understand that, don't you think God's aware of it, too? Remember, God's all about the heart.

Here's the skinny, guys. Sexual *intercourse* refers to the physical act of a man's penis entering a woman's vagina. But sex—*sex*—is the whole enchilada of erotic physical behavior with the intent to get someone aroused. I'm talking about things like oral sex, mutual masturbation, "heavy petting", and even sexy dancing (the kind that involves pelvic grinding). It's trendy these days to consider "sex" to be just the vaginal thing—while anything else up to that point is not really sex, but a harmless "hookup." But the question I'd ask is this: If it's so harmless, would you be doing it if your future wife knew? If your parents knew? Would you be doing it if Jesus were sitting beside you?

I think it's time to adjust our definitions. Once you get to deep, open-mouthed kissing (making out), the next activities on the ladder become a form of sexual behavior. Maybe they're not intercourse, but they're sex all the same. Oral sex? That's sex with a mouth. Dry thrusting until orgasm? That's sex with clothes on. Freak dancing and genital grinding? That's sex with clothes on set to music. It's all sex. If you've done those things, maybe you haven't yet had intercourse, but it's time to face the facts: You've had sex.

Q: *Does the Bible say not to have sex before you get married?*

A: Honestly, there's not a specific verse in the Bible that says, "Thou shalt not have sex before thou art married." We've made such a big deal of it that you'd think the issue was cut-and-dried, but it's not. So how do we back up all the "True Love Waits" and pledge card stuff? We do it by reading the whole Bible and using our minds to put two and two together. To start, God said that a man should leave his parents and "cleave" to his wife (i.e., have sexual intercourse), and this act makes them one flesh. It's implied here that the act of "cleaving" should be something that happens *only* with the wife, and no one else. Thus, a guy should be a virgin until he scores a wife (i.e., when he gets married). Same goes for a girl. In fact, there's a passage in Deuteronomy that says a woman who is not a virgin when she gets married should be stoned to death (Deuteronomy 22:21). Yikes. That's one rule I'm glad we no longer follow.

In any event, the Old Testament is pretty clear that both men and women were expected to remain virgins until they become husband and wife. The New Testament backs this up with passages that condemn "sexual immorality" (NIV) or "fornication" (KJV). These include 1 Corinthians 6:18 and 10:8, Ephesians 5:3, and Colossians 3:5.

Q: *Wait a second, Mr. Smarty Pants. "Sexual immorality" is a pretty vague term. It could be lots of things, right? How do you know it refers to premarital sex?*

A: Good question. I'm a lot like you. It's not enough for some dude to say, "The Bible says to 'flee from sexual immorality,' and that means no premarital sex." The whole time, I'm wondering, *Who decided "sexual immorality" included premarital sex?* That's really just our own translation, right? If it truly means "no premarital sex," then why doesn't God just come right out and make it clear? The truth is, the Bible is a weird book. It was written by a bunch of different people at different times, hundreds of years apart. But as a whole, it was inspired by God, and we can gain wisdom from it by looking at it in its entirety—rather than relying on single verses to construct a set of rules. Sure, a clean-cut verse about sex before marriage would make things easier, but maybe God prefers that we switch on our brains now and then. For instance, did you know that there's no point-blank definition of the Trinity—that the Father, Son, and Holy Spirit are One—in the Bible? In fact, the word *trinity* never shows up *anywhere* in the Old or New Testament. Yet that's a doctrine Christians strongly believe in, because we can see that it's clearly supported by various passages throughout the Bible. Same goes for God's desire for us to abstain from sex until we're married.

In the Bible, *sexual immorality* can refer to a bunch of different things, from *adultery* (having sex with another person's spouse, or cheating on your own spouse) to *incest* (having sex with a close relative) to *bestiality* (sex with an animal). In 1 Corinthians 6:9, Paul takes care to distinguish sexual immorality from adultery. The author of Hebrews does the same: "Marriage should be honored by all, and the marriage bed kept pure, for God will judge the adulterer and all the sexually immoral" (13:4). This separates adultery from "regular" immorality—both of which can keep the marriage bed from being pure—so we know immorality includes more than just adultery. And since premarital sex is forbidden in other parts of the Bible, we're safe to assume that it's wrapped up in the whole idea of "sexual immorality." Got it?

If you're still skeptical, I understand. That's cool. For lots of guys, it's enough for me to tell you the Bible says don't have sex until you're married. Other guys want proof and will accept that statement only if I can back it up with Scripture. And some guys still need something more, something more practical and concrete. The next question for them is . . .

Q: *Any non-Bible reasons I should wait to have sex?*
A: Yep. Plenty.

Big Reason Number One: Your health. Just like you swap slobber while making out, you're exchanging bodily gunk when you have sex with someone. Sexually transmitted diseases (STDs) are a big deal. There are more than 240 of them, from nasty exterior problems like herpes, pubic lice (crabs), and genital warts (yep, warts that grow on and around your penis), to bacterial diseases like syphilis and chlamydia that can mess up your insides. Then there's HIV/AIDS, which can kill you. Lots of people may have STDs but don't know it. Others may just refuse to tell anyone about it. If you sleep with enough people, your chances go way up for contracting an STD, because pretty much you're having sex with that person and every other hookup she's ever had. And one more thing: If you think oral sex keeps you safe from getting stuff, you're flat-out wrong. Diseases can be transmitted orally as well as through straight-up intercourse.

Big Reason Number Two: Your honeymoon. When my wife was young, she spent one December snooping around her house, looking for Christmas presents in her parents' usual hiding places. She found them all, and by the time the holiday rolled around, she already knew exactly what she was getting. She'll still tell you today that was the worst Christmas she ever had. Sex is a lot like Christmas, in that anticipation and excitement are a major part of the thrill. And your eventual honeymoon—whether it's five, ten, or twenty years from now—should be all about the thrill. If you're both virgins, it'll be an amazing time of sexual discovery. But if you've already done it all—if you've peeked at any of the presents before Christmas, so to speak—it'll be nothing more than an expensive vacation at the beginning of your marriage. There will be plenty of sex involved, of course, but very little will be *new*. Any time you engage in sexual activity with your girlfriend, it decreases the thrill factor of your honeymoon.

And I'm not just talking about vaginal intercourse. I'm talking about the full round of sexual behavior. Whether it's you touching her breast or vagina, her touching your penis or scrotum, the two of you engaging in oral sex, or even seeing each other naked—there will never be another first time. The very best honeymoons are the ones that are filled with first times. And the best way to make sure that happens is to remain a virgin until the honeymoon.

Big Reason Number Three: More than ever before, abstinence is cool. Back when I was in junior high and high school, no one ever even said the word *abstinence*. It just wasn't in our vocabulary. It's not like everyone was out having sex all the time, it's just that the concept of abstinence wasn't a part of teenage culture. Thankfully, it is now. Putting sex off until you're older and more mature is an accepted choice these days, even for nonreligious people. It's a way to show you're not just a stupid, follow-the-herd teenage guy who only makes decisions from beneath his pants. It's a way to show that you have principles and values and a mind of your own. There's nothing fringe anymore about waiting—it's a way to stand out from the crowd.

STEP TO MANHOOD #52

Deciding to hold off on sex until you're married, and sticking to that commitment no matter how tempting things get.

Q: *Still, it's hard to stay pure, and I screwed up last week. My girlfriend and I went too far. What do I do?*

A: Blowing it sexually is hard. *Real* hard. God is holy, and his holiness is a tough thing to weigh ourselves against. When you fail in this arena, the guilt can be huge. You can feel like a complete hypocrite, like you've not only messed things up with your girlfriend, but with God, too. Fortunately, God understands we're human. He knows we make mistakes. Our holy God is also a God of screwups and losers and guys who completely lose their minds once things start heating up. The Bible says God is slow to anger and quick to forgive. He'll love you regardless of what you've done. And one of his favorite things is helping his children get back up on their feet after they fall. God's into second chances.

But he'll also require you to face the consequences, which may include things worse than guilt—like an unplanned pregnancy or an STD. In that case, you've got some tough choices to make. If that's the case, once you're right with God you're gonna need to find an adult you can trust and ask them for help. That won't be fun, but a pregnant girlfriend or a terrible disease isn't something you want to handle on your own.

CHAPTER 10

WOMEN:
MYSTERIES EXPLAINED

Another Pop Quiz

You're hanging out with one of your really good friends, who happens to be a girl. She stands in front of you, wearing a normal-looking outfit. She looks fine in it. Actually, she looks pretty hot. You're trying not to stare. Then she asks: "Do I look fat in this?" What do you do?

a. Dutifully give her the once-over, then say, "Nope. You look fine."

b. Say "hmmmmm" as if thinking about it, squint a little, ask her to turn around a few times, then say, "Nope."

c. Honesty being the foundation of every successful friendship, tactfully nod your head after looking her over. Say, "Yes. In fact, that does make you look a little hippy."

d. Shout out a strong "No!" before she's even finished asking the question. Try to sound annoyed she'd even ask such a stupid thing.

If you answered anything other than d, then this chapter is for you. Why? Because you're clueless about women. Now, I'm no expert on the subject, but there's at least one thing I'm sure about: You never, ever tell a girl she's fat. You never imply it. You don't even appear to think about it. Just say *no*. Say it loud. Say it strong. Even if it's true, even if she looks like she just ate Rhode Island, you have to lie. That's the only time it's okay. *Do I look fat?* NO!

I love women. Love 'em. I'm married to a beautiful one who's funny and athletic and a little weird. I'm a daddy to a little girl who's equally funny and equally weird and absolutely adorable. I'm a brother to a cool, funky, intelligent sister who's a poet. She's also weird. Some of my best hanging-out friends in high school were girls. Some of my best friends today are women. I love females.

But do I understand them? Not on your life. Which puts me precisely in the same position as every man in the universe. To guys—young and old, rich and poor, experienced and inexperienced alike—women are complete mysteries.

That said, the purpose of this chapter is to explain a few things to you about girls and what makes them tick. Which makes this the most difficult collection of sentences I've ever had to string together. Wish me luck.

WHAT GIRLS ARE GOING THROUGH

You think puberty is hard for guys, what with all the erections and wet dreams and chipmunky voices? Don't be a sissy. Guys have it easy compared to the puberty train ridden by teenage girls. Consider the following:

HER BREASTS

What if the thing most girls were attracted to about guys was the size of your penis? And what if the world could get a very clear idea of your penis size just by looking at your clothed crotch? And what if everyone knew you were going through puberty because they could tell your package was getting bigger and fuller every day? And what if every time you talked face-to-face with a girl you kept noticing her eyes drop to zipper-level? What if the first thing any girl noticed (and remembered) about you was the relative length and girth of Little Junior?

Such is the life of a teenage girl. When girls hit puberty, they start to develop breasts, *and everybody knows it*. Teenage guys notice. They stare. They talk about it and snicker to themselves and construct elaborate fantasies. Then they stare some more. Teenage girls are growing breasts—about which they are very, very self-conscious—yet they're surrounded by a bunch of boob-obsessed boys. You think that's cool? Fun? It's not.

Guys have it easy. Our biggest puberty change is safely tucked inside our pants. Unless we're sporting a Speedo or dancing in the *Nutcracker* (yeah, pun intended), nobody has any idea what we look like down there.

But that's not true for girls and their breasts. When girls start getting bigger, guys can tell.

To top it off, a girl's breasts get sore as they develop. They hurt. Sometimes they grow lopsided, and a girl might have one that's bigger than the other for a while. Sometimes a girl's breasts develop early, making her stand out among her friends. Sometimes a girl gets her breasts way late in her teens, and *she* stands out among her friends for being small. Then she watches TV or checks out the annual swimsuit issue and sees all these women with mongo boob jobs, and she can't help but compare herself to them. She may be beautiful, but no way can she stack up to a surgically enhanced supermodel.

And did I mention that I'm told it's uncomfortable to wear a bra? And that it's also uncomfortable to *not* wear a bra?

Here's the point: You might think breasts are the best thing ever, but for a girl, they can be pretty annoying. It's hard to have boobs in a society that's obsessed with them.

> **THE REAL DEAL:**
> What's the only thing harder than enduring puberty as a guy? Going through puberty as a girl.

HER PERIOD

Women have ovaries. Ovaries produce an egg. Once every cycle, the egg travels down a woman's fallopian tube into the uterus, where it lays low for a few days waiting to get busy with a tall, dark, and handsome sperm. Meanwhile, the uterus has prepared a cushiony lining for the egg—a love nest, so to speak—to keep it safe for the next few days. During intercourse, a man's sperm travels into a woman's body looking to hook up with the egg in the uterus (this is called fertilization). Soft music plays. The lights dim in the love nest. It's all very romantic. And really, really dark. Then, if everything works out, the woman becomes pregnant. But if no sperm show up—or if sperm *do* show but fertilization does not occur—the egg gets flushed out of the system. Along with the spongy lining. It looks like blood, it lasts for several days, and sometimes it hurts. It's called menstruation, but it's better known as a period.

Here's what you need to know: Periods are a major pain. You think an erection is hard to hide? What about a mess of blood suddenly leaking out between your legs? If a girl's not prepared when her period hits, things can *really* become panicville. And preparing for it means keeping all sorts of absorbent stuff like tampons or maxipads in her purse or backpack or locker. Since periods last for a number of days, it's not just a temporary discomfort, either.

It's long-term. Put on a pair of tight briefs, then stuff a washrag between your legs. Then put your jeans on. Walk around like that for a week. *That's* what it feels like to manage a period.

And we haven't even gotten into PMS, which can result in headaches, bloating, nausea, zit invasions, irritability, stress—you name it (keep reading for more on the joys of PMS). Seriously, guys ought to thank God every day that we don't have to go through anything even close to menstruation.

HAIR

In the U.S., we're into hairless women. So when American girls hit puberty—when hair begins to sprout in new places—it's time to kick the hair removal into gear. Like guys, girls grow darker, coarser hair on their legs, under their arms, and in their pubic area during puberty. But unlike guys, they've gotta take a lot of that new hair off. For a guy, shaving your chin and neck may be difficult, but it doesn't compare at all to shaving your armpit. Armpits are soft and tender and highly nickable.

And sure, guys have a lot of face to shave, but that acreage doesn't compare to shaving two whole legs.

That's not all. When it comes to shaving the bikini zone, guys have *nothing* to compare to. Don't stare (or drool), but next time you see a teenage girl or a woman wearing a bikini bottom, keep in mind that a lot of the exposed skin in the pubic area naturally grows hair. And because it looks smooth to you, they very likely had to shave it. Or pluck it. Or wax it, which is pretty much like pulling it all out at once. Ouch.

That, my friends, is reason number three to respect women. The female puberty experience can be just as difficult—if not more so—than what guys go through.

WHAT'S UP ON THE INSIDE

In a lot of respects, teenage girls are not that much different from guys when it comes to their interior life—what's going on inside them. They worry about being accepted by their friends. They want to be liked. They want to be understood. They want to be happy and fulfilled. Those aren't just female desires. They're human desires, and we all have them.

Some of the thoughts, however, that regularly pop up in the female brain are unique to girls. Girls think about stuff that hardly ever crosses the male brain. To recognize some of these ideas—and to anticipate them—is one of the keys to understanding what it's like to be a teenage girl in our culture. I'm going to list three of the biggies here for you. But, first, a word of warning. These are major generalizations, which means they're true for many girls, but not all of them. Every girl is different, and so is her brain.

A GIRL IS RARELY SATISFIED WITH THE WAY SHE LOOKS

Check out any fashion or celebrity magazine aimed at women, and notice how many appearance-oriented articles are hyped on the cover:

➤ "Zap Your Zits for Good"
➤ "How to Become a Knockout for That Special Guy"
➤ "The Key to Jaw-Dropping Abs"

These headlines are usually accompanied by a photo of a model who's so hopelessly thin and attractive, no real girl will ever be able to look like her. For women in our society, the pressure is on to look good. All the time. Obsession with beauty has become a big-time problem.

"When girls get together, they talk about what they hate about themselves," a youth worker in her early twenties recently told me. "It was that way when I was in school and it's that way now. There's no end to the comparisons. Girls are almost always insecure about what they look like." Girls, she said, are constantly weighing the way they look against someone else. Maybe it's the hot cheerleader the guys ogle at the football games. Maybe it's Britney Spears or Jennifer Aniston. Doesn't matter. Because the hot cheerleader? She's insecure, too. She wishes she had a prettier face. She wishes she had slimmer hips or a firmer butt. She's just as unhappy as the rest. Teenage girls, by and large, are more concerned than guys with the way they look.

What it means for a guy. Two things. First, you should never, *ever*, joke with a girl about her appearance. Don't joke about it with her, or with her friends—because eventually she'll hear about it. She may be the best-looking woman you ever laid eyes on, but do not assume she knows it or believes it. I can't stress this enough. *Do not ever* make a negative comment about the way a girl looks. Because ten years from now, she'll still remember it. And she'll remember the way it made her feel, too.

Second, you should compliment a girl every chance you get, especially if you're on a date (but in non-dating situations, too). Just as a negative comment lasts forever, so does a positive one. A

> **BIG TIP:**
>
> A guy should never ever make a negative comment—whether teasing or not—about the way a girl looks. She'll take it very seriously, and remember it forever.

sincere compliment can make a girl's day. Tell her she has great hair or beautiful eyes and you've made her week. When you pick her up for a formal dance, tell her she looks stunning. Do *not*, on the other hand, "compliment" her by dropping a sexist or inappropriate comment. "Dude, nice rack" is not a flattering remark.

A GIRL IS LOOKING FOR ROMANCE, NOT SEX

Like guys, girls want to make an emotional connection with someone, and dating is a great way to do it. But unlike most guys, girls are not as heavily focused on the sexual aspect of dating. While many guys may be in it to get as far as they can physically, many girls are trying to gain emotional fulfillment. Guys may be hoping for a grabby makeout session, while girls are hoping only to hold hands on the way back to the car after the movie. And a girl with a rep for being sexually active? She may actually be using the sex to get the romance. For girls, sex can be a means to an end, a path to the knight in shining armor who'll sweep her off her feet. For a lot of guys, sex can be, well, pretty much just the end.

What it means for a guy. It means you need to stop being an average guy. The average, schlong-controlled guy is lame. If being average means obsessing about sex, then you need to be *above* average. Put those urges in your back pocket and sit on them for a while, then consider someone else's needs before your own. If you're in a dating relationship, take the initiative to show affection. That means doing the small, nonsexual stuff— holding her hand, opening doors for her, putting your arm around her, kissing her lightly on the cheek. Take it slow. There is nothing more annoying to a girl than a guy who starts wagging his tongue all over her when all she wanted was a simple, romantic kiss good night.

STEP TO MANHOOD #31

Considering someone else's needs before your own.

It also means that any guy-girl connection—whether it's a friends-only kind of thing or a dating relationship—should be more about the conversation and relationship-building than about the physical stuff. She's looking for the sparks that fly when you show interest in who she is and what she thinks. She wants to know that the two of you really connect with each other. Besides talking to her, another way to achieve this is through small, thoughtful gestures, especially if you're dating. Write little notes to her. Plan creative dates. Above all, do whatever it takes to make her feel special.

A GIRL KNOWS WHAT YOU'RE UP TO

Have you ever heard of something called "women's intuition"? It's the idea that while men make decisions based on logic and rational thought, women rely more on their feelings and gut instincts. The crazy thing about it is that those instincts are often right. It's been scientifically documented that girls catch subliminal messages faster and more accurately than guys do. That means they're much more perceptive about what's going on around them. They can tune in to a person's emotional state, tendencies, desires, intentions—you name it—way before a guy can. Women can read people and situations much better than men.

What it means for a guy. It means you can't get away with stuff around girls. You probably won't be able to disguise the fact that you're mad about something around a girl who knows you well. You can't hide disappointment, stress, or fear. She'll pick up on the body language.

There are other things you can't hide, either. Think you sneaked a peek down her shirt when she leaned over in class? Guess again. You may have gotten your own private peep show, but she knows you looked. I don't know how they do it, but girls know when guys are checking them out. They may let your eyes linger on their boobs or butt without calling you on it (maybe they like the attention?), but don't think you're getting away with anything. You're not.

> **BIG TIP:**
>
> You may think you're Mr. Subtlety, but girls are aware when you're checking them out.

COMMON MISCONCEPTIONS ABOUT GIRLS

Sorry, guys, but I'm about to burst a few bubbles. Most guys are dragging around a trailerload of myths, delusions, and outright fabrications about females. We think we're experts. We think we know everything. Unfortunately, we're wrong. Time to get the facts straight. Here are a few common misconceptions guys have about girls:

Misconception: Women are always a hiccup or two away from crying.

Reality: No, they're not. As we mentioned in the very first chapter, it's physically easier for girls to cry than it is for guys. And, unlike guys, girls are not regularly beaten over the head with the unspoken rule that emotions are to be stifled. In female culture, it's okay to be emotional. Crying is no big.

But are girls just sitting around all the time on the brink of tears? No. My wife cries more easily than I do, but she hates to cry. During a sad movie, she's been known to distract herself *in order to keep herself from crying.* Why? Number one, she thinks crying scrunches up her face and makes her look weird (she's wrong, of course; she looks fine as a crier). And number two, crying smears her eye makeup. My wife is not alone. Just because they can doesn't mean girls are walking around looking for a chance to switch on the waterworks. They're not scheming to use tears to manipulate guys. Crying can come easily to a girl, but it's not like that's always a good thing.

Misconception: All women are irritable and emotionally unstable during their "time of the month."

Reality: Wrong again, Jethro. The truth is, all kinds of strange symptoms and emotions have been associated with PMS (PreMenstrual Syndrome) over the years. No one's really sure what causes these symptoms, but almost everyone agrees that during the second half of the menstrual cycle, some women just don't feel like themselves. PMS sufferers have experienced physical discomfort in the form of headaches, abdominal cramps, muscle spasms, breast tenderness, bloating, constipation, or diarrhea, even acne flareups. And on the mental side of things, PMS has been known to cause anxiety, depression, hostility, fatigue, and paranoia.

Lots of girls go through some form of PMS. A small percentage meet up with the whole enchilada of bad stuff, and "that time of the month" is something they truly dread. It can be misery. Others have it relatively easy, and the only thing they have to deal with is the actual menstruation part. Most females fall

> **THE REAL DEAL:**
>
> Just because a girl may be irritable or stressed, it doesn't always mean it's her time of the month. For some girls, PMS is a major deal. But for others, it's no big whup.

somewhere in between. The thing to remember is this: Just because a girl seems upset or angry or otherwise short-tempered, *it does not mean she's getting her period.* Maybe she's just having a bad day. Maybe she just doesn't feel good. Maybe you're just being obnoxious. PMS has long been the designated scapegoat for any kind of unsatisfactory female behavior. But it shouldn't be. A girl needs to be free to think you're a dork without you blaming it on her time of the month.

Misconception: If a girl wears sexy clothes, it means she's slutty. Or horny. Or interested in me.

Reality: Time for a cold shower, Sparky. You're way off-base. Girls don't dress provocatively (low-rise jeans, exposed bellies, tight-fitting tops, skirts with slits up to *here*) because they're sluts. No, they dress that way to get attention. We mentioned earlier that girls are looking for emotional fulfillment from guys, as opposed to physical (sexual) fulfillment. One way for a girl to scratch that emotional itch is to get a guy to notice her. Girls enjoy feeling special. They like to be flirted with. They like to catch your eye. And because guys are so easily caught by the eyes—once we get a glimpse of tan, smooth, normally hidden skin, we can hardly look away—girls know their appearance is a prime way to set the hook. Just because a girl dresses sexily, however, does not mean she wants to have sex with you. It doesn't mean she is morally loose. It doesn't mean she is cheap or easy. It probably just means she's longing for attention. She wants you to notice her. Is that a smart move? Not really. Is it honoring to God? Perhaps not. But it's not an invitation for you to get frisky, either.

Misconception: Girls are only into jocks, or guys with cool cars, or guys with money.

Reality: Girls are into all kinds of guys. Varsity quarterbacks and science geeks. Soccer studs and debate dudes. Popular, outgoing guys and quiet, mysterious guys. Guys who drive Mustangs and guys who drive ancient Merkurs.

Some girls can be as shallow and appearance-minded as guys can, but most women—as we've said before—are deeper than that. They're wanting to be swept off their feet by a caring, thoughtful, romantic guy. If that guy also happens to be all muscly and handsome, then great. But if that guy is not your typical beefcake, that's also cool. You don't have to be Brad Pitt. You don't have to be rich. You don't have to drive a nice car (as long as you keep it clean). All you have to do is be confident, kind, and interested in who she is—and not *just* what she looks like.

PART THREE

SOUL

CHAPTER 11

FAMILY

Families these days are as unique and varied as the individuals in them. You might live in a traditional family made up of a father, a mother, and a kid or two. Sociologists—scientists who study the way people interact within society—call this a "nuclear family," which sounds kind of dangerous, but isn't. For years and years, the nuclear family was the basic building block of society. There weren't too many other kinds of families out there. Occasionally you'd find a family with some extras under the same roof, like a grandmother or a grandfather, but usually people assumed the mom/dad/kid combo when they talked about family.

Things have changed over the last few decades. More parents are getting divorced, leaving Mom or Dad to raise kids alone. Some people choose to go it alone, becoming single, unmarried parents through adoption. There are single-parent families who go all *Brady Bunch* and combine to become stepfamilies.

Sometimes couples have kids together, on purpose, *without* getting married first. And more and more you have gay couples who adopt kids. Basic point? These days, families come in more flavors than ice cream.

All the different combina-

> **THE REAL DEAL:**
>
> The nuclear family used to be about the only option when it came to family types. Not so much anymore.

124

tions can be confusing, but one thing's clear: Our society is changing pretty rapidly, and so is the definition of a family. Families these days can be hard to figure out. So for our purposes here, when we talk about your family, we're talking about the people you live with—the people in your house. The bizarros you share space with, argue with, laugh with, and interact with in some form or fashion on a daily basis. That's your family.

FOUR THINGS YOU NEED TO KNOW ABOUT A FAMILY

Just because families can be all over the map, that doesn't mean there aren't a few things they have in common. Here are a few of the biggies you need to get comfy with:

1. Good or Bad, You Can't Pick Your Family

Society is made of groups that share a common bond. Sports teams come together by tryouts or drafts. Teams of workers or employees are hired based on their skills. Clubs or unions are based on mutual interests or goals. But families are unique in that you get born (or married, or adopted) into one. As a kid, you don't really get a choice. You don't necessarily get to hang out with people who like the same stuff you like, or who have personalities you can get along with. Of course, some kids win the lottery and get born into wealthy, famous, even royal families, like Princes William and Harry of England. Other kids get the short end of the stick, and are born into less-than-ideal situations like poverty, abuse, or neglect. Hopefully, your family falls somewhere between those good and bad extremes.

2. Families Work Best If You Try to Get Along

I know what you're thinking: *Duh*. And I admit it—that's not the most profound statement in the world. But it's still worth bringing to the table. The hardest part about living with other people is learning how to deal with them. Throw a bunch of different personalities and interests and priorities and ages into one house, and you're bound to get some conflict. Every family has its share of problems. Family members disappoint, hurt, and disagree with one another because we're all human and we all screw up from time to time. No relationships are glitch-free, but when a relationship involves seeing each other on a daily basis and living under the same roof, then the little glitches can get big. Fast. So to make a family situation work—to be able to function without, say, biting one another's heads off—each member of the family has to learn a few important concepts. Like *compromise* (giving in on stuff in order to settle differences). Or *empathy* (trying to identify with another person's feelings or perspective). And *respect* (showing appreciation and honor).

> **BIG TIP:**
>
> Every family goes through disagreements, but the families that get past them do so via compromise, empathy, and respect.

Combine those with open, honest communication, and problems are easier to beat.

3. Family Relationships Are Always Changing

You might not remember it, but when you were a baby, you were extremely close to your parents. You relied on them for everything—feeding you, keeping you warm, making sure you weren't lurching around in poop-loaded Huggies. Then you got older. You became more independent. And now you're a teenager and ready to think for yourself. You want more freedom, and the parentals are having a hard time letting go. They don't love you any less, of course, but it seems lately there's been more friction than ever before. Maybe your dad seems completely out of touch. Maybe your mom seems way too overprotective or invasive. The culprit? Change. You've changed. And as a result, your parents have changed, too. You're on different pages. But guess what? In a few years you'll change again. The stuff Mom does won't annoy you so much. You'll become better friends with your dad than you ever thought possible. That's because family relationships move in cycles. They're always shifting, depending on what's happening in each of your lives. The trick is to stick it out through the tough times so you can enjoy the really good times.

4. The Best Parts of Your Life Will Probably Involve Your Family

My little sister got married this summer in Colorado, and everyone in our immediate family was there. Our parents, both sets of grandparents (Deenie and Brownie, Memaw and PawPaw), our three aunts and one uncle, my brother and his family, and my wife and our two kids. We all hung out for a few days, talking and fly-fishing and hiking around and watching the kids play. It ended with a simple wedding in a mountain meadow near a trickling stream. We had a blast. I can say the same thing about my own wedding and my brother's wedding and the births of each of our children. And then there are all the holidays and the birthdays and the graduations and all the camping and snow-skiing and fishing trips we've taken over the years. When I think back to the really good times in my life, there always seemed to be family members around. Despite some of the junk we go through, a family will usually give us all we need to enjoy life: love, acceptance, support, encouragement, protection, and hope. Without those things, life is hard. Life is hard anyway. The role of a family is to soften it a little.

DEALING WITH
THE MAJOR HARD STUFF

Your family sounds really perfect and loving, you may be thinking. *But what about my family? Life at my house isn't all hugs and kisses and mountain meadows and grandparents named Deenie. You don't know what I'm going through.*

You're right. I don't. The truth is, kids who grow up in happy, loving homes are lucky. Not everyone has a great home life. Not everyone has fond memories of family time. Not everyone can rely on the people in their house to give them love and support and all those positive things. Here are a few tips on how to handle some of the more difficult home situations:

THE SITUATION: DIVORCE

What's Hard About It: You're going from a two-parent home to a one-parent home. That can mean a number of different things. You might have to move or change schools or get used to living in two different places, depending on how custody works out. You might have to deal with money issues, if suddenly your mom has to get a job to pay the bills or if all the legal expenses have taken a chunk out of the family budget. You'll have to adjust to not seeing one of your parents as often as you used to. And you'll have to wade through a lot of hurt feelings and anger your parents might be lobbing at each other.

The Main Thing You Can Do: The number one thing you need to do to get through a divorce is stop imagining ways you might have prevented it. It's not your fault, so stop blaming yourself for it. That's a natural reaction—at some point, all children of divorce think they're to blame—but it's absolutely untrue. It's as wrong as Michael Jackson's nose. Parents divorce because of problems they have with each other, not with you.

Other Things You Can Do: *Keep your routine.* One of the best ways to deal with major change is to keep everything else as normal as possible. Keep to the same schedule, keep hanging with the same friends, keep doing what you've been doing. Stay involved.

Try not to take sides. Again, this is a problem between your parents, so it's not up to you to decide who's right. You need the freedom to relate to one parent without the other getting all weird about it. Do your best to stay impartial.

Maintain communication. If you end up staying with one parent a majority of the time, make sure you keep in touch with the other. For parents, one of the hardest things about divorce is not being able to see their kids whenever they want. By keeping your mom or dad up-to-date with what's going on in your life, you're helping them handle the heartbreak.

Find someone to talk to. The worst thing you can do during a divorce is bottle up all your stress and confusion and depression. Let it loose. Talk to someone about it: one of your parents, an older sibling, a teacher, a youth leader, or even a friend who's gone through the same experience. You'll feel better once you've vented, and maybe they'll be able to help you work through some of the tough stuff.

THE SITUATION: A BLENDED FAMILY

What's Hard About It: The blending itself. A blended family occurs when a parent remarries, and you end up living with a nonbiological stepparent (and possibly a kid or two of theirs). You're basically combining two families into one, thus the "blending." Unfortunately, families aren't like smoothies. You can't just dump a bunch of ingredients into a house and expect them to mush all together into something fun and healthy and delicious. The truth is, you're always going to be a unique individual, connected to your original family and parents. That's why blending is especially hard when you're a teenager.

The Main Thing You Can Do: Be patient. You're entering into a new family with new members and new rules and new relationships. It's gonna take time for things to settle. If other kids are involved, you won't be comfortable around them for months. It'll take even longer to get used to a new parent. You're living in a new world—one you probably wouldn't have chosen for yourself. So you have two options. You can go all teenagery about it and pout and be disrespectful and act like a jerk. Or, you can be a man and hold steady, believing that things will work themselves out. Pick option two. Be flexible. Learn to compromise. Try to be understanding. It gets better.

> **BIG TIP:**
>
> All the weird stuff that comes with a blended family will, in most cases, eventually get better. Your job is to be patient until that happens.

Other Things You Can Do: *Be fair.* If one of your parents is getting remarried, it probably means you've gone through a divorce or, worse, the death of a parent. Either case means some combination of grief and anger and a huge amount of change. It's easy to take that anger or depression out on someone else—especially if there's an obnoxious new stepsibling or a stepparent you can hardly relate to. But beating them up because *you're* upset is not fair to anyone involved.

Look for the positive. Maybe you're an only child who finally has a brother or sister to hang with. Maybe your new stepdad has a big house or a pool or a rockin' stereo system. Maybe your new stepmom will help your dad become himself again after all the heartache he's gone through. It seems impossible, but blended families can often bring as much good into your life as bad. You just have to look for it.

Communicate. Seems like we mention communication on every page, but there's a reason for that: It's the most important ingredient to healthy relationships. Your new family will come with new rules, personalities, and routines. The best way to work through them is to make sure everyone's in agreement on the major stuff. That means you're gonna have to talk some things out. Be a man and do it.

THE SITUATION: ABUSE

What's Hard About It: It's all hard. That goes without saying.

The Main Thing You Can Do: *Recognize it.* The first step to getting out of an abusive situation is to recognize and admit you're in one. Experts say one out of every one hundred teens are being abused. They identify several different kinds of abuse. The most common for guys is probably physical abuse—hitting, beating, choking, whatever. It's the kind that causes physical injury to you. Other types of abuse may be *sexual* (inappropriate contact between an adult and child), *emotional* (when yelling and anger go way *way* too far, beyond any sort of healthy communication), and *neglect* (when the basics of life—like food, clothing, shelter, and emotional support—are withheld). If you've grown up with any of these things or lived with them for a long time, it may be hard to admit there's a problem. You might think that's how all families act. *It's not.* There's nothing normal or acceptable about any kind of abuse.

The Other Main Thing You Need to Do: *Get help.* It may be the hardest thing you'll ever have to do, but you have to tell someone—a teacher, a doctor, a leader at church, or someone else in your family. Anyone you can trust. (You can also call Childhelp USA toll-free at 1-800-422-4453.) The point is, you need to get someone else involved. Once you've identified abuse, you need to take the next step toward changing the situation. Telling someone about it is step one. They'll help you report it to the proper authorities, then they'll help you find a way to get out of it, if necessary. They'll also make sure you know you're not alone.

Some teens choose to endure abuse silently. Maybe they're embarrassed about it, or they think the problem is hopeless. They're wrong. There's no reason to go through that stuff. If you think you might be in an abusive situation—or if one of your friends might be in an abusive situation—you need to tell someone about it. Now. Put this book down.

DEALING WITH THE MINOR HARD STUFF

The difficulties our families face aren't always major life-changers like divorce or remarriage. Thank God they're not always criminal activities like abuse. Sometimes we deal with smaller issues, like an insufferable sister or a parent with a short leash. But small issues are important, too, because that's how every big issue starts. The trick is to identify them when they're small and weak and relatively harmless, then to do whatever it takes to get rid of it. Earlier we mentioned three important concepts family members need to learn and practice to keep from going at one another like a pack of wild hyenas. Those were *compromise, empathy,* and *respect.* They are your tools for destroying the minor problems. How do you put them to use? Keep reading.

COMPROMISE

Conflicts develop when two people have different needs or desires. To satisfy the needs of one means another person's needs go unfulfilled. Compromise finds a way to make both parties happy. Here's how it works. Let's say you've reached driving age. Mom and Dad—being the absolute best parents in the world—have found some hand-me-down clunker of a car for you (my first car was a two-tone dirt-brown 1977 Chevrolet Caprice Classic). The car is yours, they say, but you have to find a way to pay for the gas and half the insurance. So you get a job, right? Right, except Mom stipulates that between school and church and soccer and band and your fantasy football league, you're already way too busy to hold down a regular job. She's afraid your schoolwork will suffer.

"But, Mom!" you say (not realizing that any sentence starting with "But, Mom" is nails on a chalkboard to your mother). "I'm sixteen years old!"

To you, the logic is simple. You want to drive. And to drive, you've

gotta work. You're in a no man's land: drive/work vs. study. Which will it be? Picking one over the other will make one of you happy, but it'll also make the other mad. The solution is to compromise—to give and take in order to find a solution that's good for both of you.

In this example, a meaningful compromise is to step away from one of your activities. If your fantasy football league is taking up several hours every Saturday for research and administrative work, drop it like pocket lint. That'll free up a big chunk of time you can use to make some gas money without taking away from your schoolwork. You're happy because now you can tool around in the ancient Caprice. Dude, you rock. And Mom's happy because you're not giving up study time to do it. That's compromise, and it's one of the most powerful conflict-resolution tools out there.

EMPATHY

There's an old saying that goes like this: *Don't criticize a person until you've walked a mile in their shoes.* Now, I've seen guys' shoes. I've smelled guys' shoes. And I can tell you without hesitation that there's no way you can get me to even *try* your doghouses on, much less hike in them. That said, there is a lot of validity to the statement—you have no right to harsh on someone until you've looked at things through their eyes. That's called empathy.

You're going out with friends on a Friday night. Mom wants you back in the house by 11:30, on the dot. Your friends are gonna be out until at least midnight, so you feel like a total dope because you're the early bird. So here you are again with two choices. *One*, you can think only of yourself. That's the easy road. Not quite the God-honoring choice, and it'll lead to a fight with Mom.

Or *two*, you can strap on Mom's sandals. Consider her point of view. For instance, your mom knows she won't be able to sleep until all of her kids—which means you—are home safe in their beds. Mom also knows that most juvenile crime and/or drinking and/or sexual activity occurs after 12 a.m. That doesn't mean she thinks you're gonna get all criminal at the stroke of midnight. It just means she doesn't trust your friends. Getting you home early reduces the chance she'll have to bail you out of the juvie at some point. And, in her mind, a curfew helps you learn to follow and respect rules, even if you don't like them. Which is a very adult thing to learn. Getting home on time proves you can be trusted.

Empathy is a valuable behavior to practice, because it leads to understanding. Your family may sometimes seem like aliens. Put on their shoes occasionally, and they'll still seem like aliens. But at least you'll understand *why*. That's what empathy does: It delivers the *why*.

STEP TO MANHOOD #50

Walking a mile in someone else's shoes (figuratively speaking, of course) before busting out the criticism.

RESPECT

Respect comes from the same tree as empathy. It means understanding that family members—even parents—are humans, too, and they deserve to be treated that way. Respect is an easier concept to grasp when we look at it from a practical standpoint. What does it look like? For one thing, showing respect means talking in a courteous way. That means communicating with family members without raising your voice, without being sarcastic or mean, without using profanity, and without an angry or accusatory tone. Showing respect means practicing politeness and good manners, even toward your cornball sister. Respect means showing consideration for privacy. It means being more concerned for others than for yourself. "Do nothing out of selfish ambition or vain conceit," the Bible says, "but in humility consider others better than yourselves. Each of you should look not only to your own interests, but also to the interests of others" (Philippians 2:3–4).

Consider a car engine. You put motor oil in the engine because, without it, the car won't work. Motor oil protects and lubricates all the moving parts. Without it, all those parts would grind against each other and your engine would come to a complete halt. Thermal breakdown. Oil keeps the engine parts clean. It keeps the engine cool. It keeps everything from falling to pieces.

Respect is the motor oil of family life. Without it, you've got friction and heat and danger and eventual destruction. With it, everything's silky smooth. To keep your family running without major breakage, step away from your own interests every once in a while and consider the interests of others.

WHAT ARE MY PARENTS THINKING?

The most incomprehensible people in the world are the ones who brought you into it: your parents. And as a teenager, when you think about family (especially family *problems*), you probably think about Mom and Dad. The most common conflicts between parents and kids don't happen because their teenage son is a bad seed or a rebellious twit. No, conflicts happen because the kid and the parents aren't always on the same page. Relationships break down due to a lack of understanding. With that in mind, here is a simple guide for understanding your parents (which, of course, leads to—everyone now—*empathy and respect*). Read it and watch your conflicts disappear!

Hmmm . . . maybe that's overstating it. Read it anyway.

1. Your Parents Love You and Want What's Best for You

This should go without saying (and often it does), but your mom and dad are crazy about you. They remember when they brought you home from the hospital . . . and when you learned to walk . . . and when you said your first words. And now that the adorable little guy in their old photos is growing up, they want you to succeed. But they also still want to protect you. They've invested thousands of thousands of hours of work and prayer into your life up to this point, and they want to make sure that investment pays out.

2. Because They Love You So Much, They Naturally Worry About You

It's not that they don't trust you or your decision-making abilities. It's that they aren't so hot on the decision-making abilities of the kids you hang with. They don't trust other drivers. They don't trust the kids at the party. They don't trust the freakish world we live in. You may be a complete Boy Scout, but Mom and Dad realize you can't control everything that happens. They can't, either. That's why they worry, and that won't ever change.

3. They're Confused About Who You Are

Raising a kid may be hard work, but the time goes by *fast.* Scary fast. To your parents, it seems like you were just learning how to talk yesterday. Now you're asking for a car. It's hard for them to accept that you're becoming a grownup.

4. They Know You're Confused About Who You Are

Your parents were teenagers once. They realize that being a teenager can be an awkward transitional phase. You're changing on a weekly basis. You're thinking more for yourself. You're forming your own beliefs and starting to challenge some of the beliefs and traditions your parents hold dear. You seem like an adult at times (like when you ask for a car on your sixteenth birthday). But you can also act like a child (like when you pout, slam your bedroom door, and give Mom and Dad the silent treatment when they *don't* give you a car). Your parents have been there. They know it's hard, but they're trying to do what it takes to help you make the transition as smoothly as possible.

5. Your Parents Screwed Up a Time or Two When They Were Your Age, and They Don't Want You to Make the Same Mistakes

Even if they learned from those mistakes, they don't want you to have to deal with the heartache that's attached. If they see you showing some of the same tendencies they experienced at your age—like hanging around with the wrong people, or being disinterested in school—then it's gonna freak

> **THE REAL DEAL:**
>
> Your parents love you. Your parents worry about you. And your parents don't want you to make the same mistakes they did.

them out. They've been there, and they don't want you to have to fight the same battles.

6. Talking to You About Stuff Like Sex Makes Them Uncomfortable

You might want to sit down for this, but your mom and dad have had a lot of sex. With each other. Compared to you, they are sex experts. They're sexperts. *Blech.* But when you were a kid, they tried to keep all the sex-having quiet, so you wouldn't ask questions you weren't ready to hear answers to. Now that you're older—now that you have questions about sex—they're a little uneasy. Sex is a personal thing. They aren't sure how much you know, or how much they should fill you in on. They have to make a transition in their thinking, and it's hard to accept that you're ready to talk about the wild monkey dance. Think *you're* uncomfortable talking to Mom and Dad about sex? It's twice as bad for them.

7. They're Responsible for You

They feel like it's up to them to make sure you grow up into a nice young man who'll represent the family well. They're responsible for making sure you get a good education. They feel like they're responsible for your spiritual development. Even bigger, they're responsible for you legally. That's right—parents can be held responsible for their kids' behavior. You do something to somebody, and Mom and Dad can be forced to pay for injuries (financial or physical) caused by whatever you did. Wreck a car and it's their dime. Destroy a mailbox and it comes out of Dad's wallet. They may also be forced to serve jail time for you. Seriously. You're responsible for yourself, of course, but some decisions you make can affect your parents. If *I* were your dad, I'd worry about that, too.

When it comes right down to it, I can only be honest and tell you that, yep, you're gonna fight with your family. You're not always going to get along, whether it's with your parents or a brother or sister. Families argue. They throw sticks and stones. Their words can hurt you more than anything, because they know you more intensely than anyone. Which is why—other than your future wife—you will never be closer to anyone in the world than the members of your family. You'll never find more love, more understanding, or more compassion than from your own flesh and blood. It's just that sometimes you have to look past a lot of nuttiness to get to it.

The best advice I can give you about family is this: Right now, try to respect them. Try to empathize. Try to understand. And above all, be patient. They're far from cool now, but when you get older, you'll like them a lot better. I promise.

CHAPTER 12

FRIENDS

A Sample Conversation
Between Two Female Friends:

Lacey: Girl, I'm not kidding. He was so checking you out.

Jenn: He was so not!

Lacey: I swear! He was. He totally was eying your butt.

Jenn: NO! Please tell me you're lying. I look like a complete whale in this. So . . . what did he think?

Lacey: He was ga-ga. Totally staring. He loooooooooves you.

Jenn: He does not!

Lacey: No, I'm, like, dead serious. He really does. He told Brad and Brad told Cameron and Cameron told Kenzie and Kenzie told me. He thinks you're hot.

Jenn: He does not! (Pause.) He is pretty cute, though.

Lacey: Cute?! Girl, puppies are cute. Sixth graders are cute. This guy is hot. He's got abs like Brad Pitt.

Jenn: No way.

Lacey: Oh, yeah.

Jenn: No way.

Lacey:	He had his shirt off at soccer practice the other day. And he was all sweaty. Total six-pack.
Jenn:	He was checking me out?
Lacey:	Totally.
Jenn:	Can you see my panty line? You sure I don't look fat?
Lacey:	You look awesome. You should talk to him.
Jenn:	Yeah, I should talk to him. I gotta go. Call me tonight?

Meanwhile, Another Conversation, This One Between Two Male Friends:

Jake:	You think she saw me?
Ryan:	What, were you checkin' out her butt?
Jake:	No.
Ryan:	Yeah, you were. Dude, she's hot anyway.
Jake:	Yeah, she is. I gotta jet. Madden tonight?
Ryan:	Whatever. Let me know. Later.

Big difference #154 between guys and girls: their friendships. A friendship between girls is typically full and open and all-encompassing. Everyone's invited to the party. Girls talk with each other about boys. Girls talk about the way they look. Girls talk about the way guys look. Girls talk about other girls. Then they talk some more about boys. Girls talk a lot.

But guys? Guy friends are different. We like to hang out with one another. We talk about sports. Maybe we talk about a TV show or a movie. But mostly we talk about one of two things—girls and video games (not necessarily in that order). And when we do talk about those subjects, the commentary is usually short, sweet, and to the point. While girls are experts at developing tight friendships

> **THE REAL DEAL:**
>
> Friendships between girls are deep, with lots of discussion and emotion. Friendships between guys are less deep, with less talking.

with each other—the kinds of friendships where they talk about *everything*, where they share deep feelings and emotions—guys tend to relate on a shallower level.

That's the way it is as teenagers, and it only gets worse from there. Unless you work really, really hard at it, most of your high-school friends will grow distant as you make the transition into college. Then you'll lose track of your college friends after *that* graduation. And if you're like most guys, there may come a time in your adult life when you look around and realize, *Huh, I don't really have any close guy friends anymore. What happened?*

That's why great friendships are so important to have when you're a teenager. You may be developing some relationships that you'll carry with you into adulthood. But you'll also be, as with so many other things, "learning the ropes" about friendship. You'll be getting the hang of it now so that once you're an adult, you'll be an expert. Let's get started.

WHY WE NEED FRIENDS

You might want to sit down, because you're about to read something that will blast your socks off. Here it is: Life is hard.

Okay, fine. Maybe that's not so much the big news flash, but it's important to remember every now and then (as if you're not reminded of it daily). The best way to get through the struggles of life—stress, school, family problems, scary world events—is to make sure you're not trying to squeak past them on your own. That's where friends come in. When the pressure's on, it's good to know there are some other guys who are dealing with the same thing and who can help you hold everything together. Besides just being around, what specific things do good friends bring to the table?

TWO GOOD EARS

You've got to be able to count on your friend to listen. Listening is especially hard for guys, because when we hear about a problem, our natural tendency is to try to solve it. Guys are great at giving advice or telling someone what to do. But receiving advice isn't

Man, I gotta vent...

always on your friend's agenda. Sometimes, people just need the chance to vent and get stuff out in the open, so they can make decisions on their own. A good, listening friend helps them along that path.

A NEW PERSPECTIVE

Back to the problem-solving thing guys do. Sometimes you can think about a problem—let's say, a disagreement with your parents—all day long, and never figure out what to do. Why? Because you're too close to the situation. You're in it too deep to look at things from any perspective besides your own. Which is severely limited. If that's the case, then a friend might be able to offer a good solution that you never would have considered. Problem solved.

ACCEPTANCE

A friend likes you because of who you are. Not because of the clothes you wear, or what kind of car you (or your parents) drive, or because of your latest grade in economics class. A friend doesn't care about the latest zit carnival on your forehead. A friend tries not to judge you. The best friends in the world are the ones who like you even when you're in one of your moods, even when you're being a jerk, even when you don't give them any reason to like you back. A friend who accepts you, no strings attached, makes it much easier for the two of you to disagree about stuff.

A TRUST VAULT

More than anything else, you've got to trust your friend. If you've been sharing with him about some crush you have on a girl, and the next thing you know that girl knows about it, having heard from her cousin who heard from her lab partner who heard it from the girl who hangs out with your best friend's sister, who heard it straight from him, then—well, you've got the right to be mad. What good is it for a friend to listen to you if you can't be totally honest with him? A good friend ought to be able to take something you said, lock it up in the trust vault, and keep it there until you say it's cool to withdraw it.

FLEXIBILITY

We hit on this in the previous chapter, but it's a fact that people change. I'm not the same guy now I was when I was eighteen. You're not the same guy now you were at twelve. Heck, by the time you finish this book, you may be different (much more sophisticated, perhaps, or tons cooler). By the time you graduate, you will have undergone a major overhaul in the way you look, think, and act. You'll have changed. A lot. If you don't want to get into the habit of making new friends every time something about you turns different—your hairstyle, your politics, your girlfriend, your classes—then finding a friend who gives you room to grow is vitally important.

WHY DEEP FRIENDSHIPS
ARE HARD FOR GUYS

This reason is so simple you're going to think it's stupid, but it's true: Guys are hesitant to develop a deep, meaningful friendship with another guy because a lot of them are afraid of being labeled a homosexual. Lots of guys are homophobic, which means having an unnatural fear or prejudice related to homosexuals or homosexuality. Some guys get so freaked out about gay people that they won't take any chance at all to develop a friendship because it carries an idiotic risk along with it—the risk that people will talk.

"Jason and Craig hang out together all the time," someone might say. "Ten bucks says they're gay."

There are two major things wrong with the sentence above. The first is the stereotype. Just because two males are close friends does not mean they are closeted Streisand fans (which is also a stereotype—my bad). If spending lots of time together turns two guys into secret lovers, then your school's basketball and football and baseball and soccer teams are full of gay guys. Because guys on sports teams spend tons of time with one another. In locker rooms. All sweaty and stuff. So that's just a dumb statement.

The second problem with the fear of being plastered with a gay label is that it prevents guys from achieving any sort of relational intimacy. And I don't mean physical intimacy, so quit sniggering. I'm talking about emotional intimacy—the ability to really open up to someone, to share a piece of your soul with them. It's truly being yourself in the presence of another person, without feeling that you have to act tough or macho or cool all the time. It's sharing who you are on the inside.

STEP TO MANHOOD #12

Developing a close friendship with another guy without being worried about the gay stigma.

The truth is, guys suck at relationships. We're afraid to open ourselves up to another person because we're way too concerned about being cool. It's hard to trust people enough to show them who you really are—the part of you that's not always cool, that's worried about the future, that feels like a dork around pretty girls. We've talked a lot about how your teenage years are a training ground for adulthood, a chance for you to learn how to make decisions and deal with people before you're in charge. Before the training wheels come off and life becomes "real." (Whatever—as if it's not real enough already.)

Friendship follows that same pattern, but not quite the way you'd think: A close friendship with another guy helps train you to be married. Here's why. A lot of guys never reach any sort of intimacy in a friendship until they meet the person they eventually marry. That's pretty sad. They miss out on the joy of having a close friend who truly knows them. And they also go into the marriage relationship trying to play catch-up. Why? Because they don't know what a deep, real relationship looks like. They've never seen one before, yet suddenly they're asked to invest all their emotions and feelings into their future wife, and it's hard. It makes the marriage start out in a hole the guy dug for himself.

That's why it's good to develop close relationships now. It'll help make your teen years more bearable, and it'll make you a better husband several years from now. And it doesn't mean you're gay!

HOW TO NOT BE A GOOD FRIEND

Earlier we mentioned several things that good friends can provide you, from a listening ear to acceptance of who you are. But if you're like me, you probably knew that stuff already. What we may not be aware of are all the things that *keep* you from good friendships, the stuff you shouldn't bring to the table.

BEING TOO COOL

Trying to be cool all the time is an excellent way to end up friendless and alone. It's not like guys stink at relationships because we have absolutely no idea what it means to be a friend. It's just because we're trying so hard to be manly we refuse to do anything that might seem uncool. Like being real. Like admitting insecurities. Like discussing how we feel. Those things are essential to friendships. I've said it before and I'll say it again: Guys, the secret to a good life is dropping the cool mask. And stepping on it. And kicking it into the street.

PUTTING PEOPLE DOWN

Guys are masters of smack. We pop a three over some dude's outstretched arms, and it's hard to resist dogging him the rest of the way down the court. We smoke a guy on PlayStation, and the verbal darts start flying. The put-down is fun on a lighthearted basis, but sometimes it can go overboard. Even if it started as kidding, when a guy gets told he shoots like a girl fourteen million times every day, he'll start to believe it. You can be called a loser only so many times before you actually *feel* like a loser. And that's bad. Enjoy your smack, but don't let it go too far. Shut it down before the teasing turns to sticks and stones.

BEING ARROGANT

It's one thing to be confident, to be so certain of who you are and what you believe that you can ignore stupid stuff, like fighting or smoking or underage drinking. Confidence is good. But arrogance is something entirely different. Being arrogant is thinking you're better than everybody else. It's

> **BIG TIP:**
>
> It's cool to be confident. It's not so cool to think you're better than everyone else. Nobody likes a guy who's full of himself.

making fun of a person because the clothes he wears aren't as trendy as yours. It's being so self-absorbed that you enjoy making life miserable for anyone who is different from you. People are naturally self-centered—it's hard to be entirely selfless—but when that self-centeredness starts to turn you into a snob, then you need to put a cap in it. Nobody likes a guy who's full of himself. Not girls. Not other guys. Not even dogs.

RESORTING TO VIOLENCE

None of us are clones. We all have minds of our own. We have opinions and beliefs and all that stuff that makes us who we are. So naturally, we're gonna disagree with one another. As

guys, though, all too often we see dis-
agreements turn nasty when it gets
physical. That's never acceptable.
Never. Violence can turn a small
problem into a disaster that affects
the rest of your life. Forget guns in
schools—you can kill a guy just by punching him wrong, or causing him to hit his
head in a fall. Think you can't just walk away
from a fight? Believe me. You can. You may never hear this said
at your school, but walking confidently away from a fight is just
as cool as winning a fight with a knockout punch. Why?
Because it makes the other guy—the guy who's all worked up
over whatever—look like a fool. He's all ready to throw down,
and you're basically just ignoring him. Walking away from a
fight is not only more manly than fighting, it's more cool. (And
it's also, I suspect, something Jesus would do.)

A FEW WORDS ABOUT CLIQUES

As a teen, you have to deal with cliques. When you get to college, you'll have to deal with cliques. Heck, as an adult, you'll
still have to deal with cliques. Cliques pop up everywhere—at
church, at work, at school, at the gym. They're a part of life, and
to be honest, they're not always a bad thing.

A clique is simply a close group of friends who share a common interest or characteristic. Maybe at your school, all the
cheerleaders are friends because they do the same stuff. Lots of
the jocks at school hang out because they're on the same team.
You have band cliques, fencing club cliques, Goth cliques, what-

ever. Since the teen years can be so uncomfortable for guys anyway—what with all the puberty and confusion and finding-out-who-I-am stuff—it's good to have friends who know what you're going through. Cliques are comforting, and that's good.

But cliques can also bring the negative. For one thing, they can turn intelligent, clear-thinking guys into brainless sheep. Guys who make the "in-crowd" may become reluctant to make decisions for themselves because they risk falling out of the same crowd. They may start to act the same as everyone else in the clique in order to fit in. There's a name for that, you know. It's called peer pressure. (Go back and reread chapter 2 for a quick refresher.)

Peer pressure is a major part of cliquedom. It causes smart guys to do dumb things. Like categorizing people unjustly—deciding someone is not cool just because he's not in the clique. Maybe it's teasing or bullying. Maybe it involves giving in to the temptation to try drugs or drinking or smoking. If you're trying to fit into a clique that pushes its members to do *that* garbage, then it's time to reboot your brain. Wake up. Sounds like the clique may not be as cool as you thought.

Which doesn't really make things that much easier, does it? Even if the in-crowd does stuff you don't really agree with, they're still the popular group, right? They're the ones the rest of the school looks to for fashion advice. They're who we cheer for at football and basketball games. The popular girls are whom we fantasize about asking to the winter formal or the prom.

But here's the question you should be asking: Why are the cool kids popular? *Answer: Because everyone keeps telling them how cool they are.* And that's why we blindly buy into it when the same kids tell us we're not cool enough to be in their orbit.

So what do you do? Become a clique-buster. The best way to counter the popular crowd is to forget about them. Ignore them. Refuse to hold them up as icons of coolness. Stick up for the people they make fun of. Do the right thing even when they don't. Be cool to your own group of friends and don't worry about whether the king and queen of the school know you exist. Quit acting like they're the bees knees (whatever that means), and pretty soon they won't be.

So does that mean you start acting like a jerk to them? No way. We're still Christians. We're still trying to show God's love to others. But we don't have to act or think just like everyone else. We don't have to play by the rules of the clique. Remember, being popular isn't any guarantee of happiness. Popular kids are still lonely. They still strive to fit in. They still worry about being accepted. They haven't solved anything. So why not just find a great group of friends you enjoy being around, rather than stressing all the time about elbowing your way into a clique?

> **BIG TIP:**
>
> The best way to bust a clique is to stop caring what its members think of you.

. . . AND A FEW WORDS ABOUT
GIRL FRIENDS

That's girl (space) friends, not girlfriends. As in friendships with the opposite sex. This has long been an issue for teenage guys and girls alike. What do you do about guy-girl friendships? How do you handle them? Because a couple of different things are gonna happen when a guy and a girl hang out in a non-dating relationship. One, you're going to get an SUV-load of questions from people about when the two of you will start going out, because it's not always considered normal for a guy to have a great female friend and not want to date her. Which brings us to number two: You end up getting interested in her as more than a friend, and the relationship starts to change. You think that won't happen? Good luck.

Back when I was in high school, some of my closest friends were girls. Maybe two or three among my school friends, and another two or three I used to hang with at church. I loved having close, opposite-sex friendships. But I also have to be honest: At one point or another, I probably thought hard about liking each one of these girls, in a more-than-friends way. I went through a series of secret crushes. As a guy, I thought it was cool to have friends who were girls, but I was never quite satisfied. I wanted the benefits a girlfriend could provide.

There's something else I should mention. One of those church girls I used to hang with? She eventually became my wife. After knowing each other as friends from the time we were both in diapers, the two of us fell in love and got married. Sometimes friendships blossom into romance, and I wouldn't have it any other way.

WHAT'S GOOD ABOUT OPPOSITE-SEX FRIENDSHIPS

Plenty. Guys can learn a ton about girls—how to talk to them, how to understand them, what floats their boat, what drives them crazy—in a safe, nonromantic environment. When you're just hanging out together, there's none of the stress or pressure of a dating scenario, and both of you are free to be yourselves. No masks. No pretending. Opposite-sex friendships provide a great way for guys to learn how to get along with girls, and for girls to learn the same about us guys.

Also on the plus side are the unique benefits that opposite-sex friendships offer. Guys enjoy hanging with girls because it's not so competitive. There's more depth to these relationships due to the talking and sharing girls like to do. And on her part, hanging out with a guy can actually be restful. She won't feel like she has to "perform" conversationally or engage in intense, emotional discussions about people and body image and all the other stuff girls talk about regularly. Sometimes a girl just wants to chill, and that's a lot easier with guys than fellow girls.

WHAT'S HARD ABOUT OPPOSITE-SEX FRIENDSHIPS

The main pitfall is the pressure to hook up. Our culture doesn't always allow guys and girls to just be friends. We want romance. We want love and fireworks and passionate music to crescendo the first time you kiss. Your friends will probably ask when the two of you will finally get together. Your family will even wonder about it. And before long, you'll have considered it yourself. The truth is, teenagers are sexual beings. You're smack in the middle of a period of mental and physical growth, during which sex starts to become a major part of life. So it's very natural that those feelings of attraction start to color the way you look at people. And if you have a close friend who is a girl, it's not unusual that one day you'll wake up and look at her in a new way. That can be exciting . . . and tough.

> **THE REAL DEAL:**
>
> Teen guys are smack in the middle of sexual development, so it's natural to suddenly look at one of your female friends in a whole new light.

So what do you do then? That's the big question. If you handle it right, the friendship-into-relationship thing can be great, because a good friendship is a great foundation for a dating relationship. You already know each other and won't have to deal with all the awkward first-date stuff. But if you handle it wrong, you may find it hard to keep the friendship as close as it once was. If you like her, but she doesn't like you back (at least not *that* way), she may feel weird about hanging out with a guy who's all crushed out on her. You may feel weird about being around a girl who rejected your romantic advances. Weirdness makes friendships hard.

Ultimately you have two choices. You can be up front and honest about it and hope she feels the same way. Or, you can keep those feelings to yourself until you know for sure whether or not she's interested. Sometimes it takes a while (it did for me and my wife). Sometimes it never happens. But if you can handle the interior pressure of liking someone secretly—and if you can keep it from messing up your existing friendship—then maybe it's worth it to keep things on the down-low until you know for sure. If your feelings persist, though, you've gotta come clean at some point. In these sorts of things, honesty is always the best policy. It may be risky, but she's your friend. And you don't want to hide stuff like that from your friends—especially if it involves them. Take a deep breath, wait for the right time, and make the plunge.

CHAPTER 13
FAITH

There's a parable in the Bible that you don't hear about as often as the other stories Jesus told. It's not as popular as, for instance, the ones about the prodigal son or the Good Samaritan. It sure doesn't show up in Sunday school songs or children's Bibles. Why? Because the parable I'm talking about doesn't make much sense. At all. It's a crazy story.

It's also my favorite story in the Bible. It's called the parable of the workers in the vineyard, from Matthew 20. Here's how it goes:

A landowner decides to hire a bunch of guys early one morning to put in a day's work at his vineyard. He promises them a full day's pay—let's say a hundred bucks. A few hours later he goes into town and sees a bunch of guys standing around with nothing to do. "Hey," he says. "Wanna earn a little money?" They do, so he puts these new guys to work in his vineyard as well. He also promises to pay *them* a fair wage. Around noon, he heads back into town and, finding some other unemployed guys, does the same thing. Mid-afternoon he hires yet another batch of workers. Finally, right before quitting time, he sees a handful of less-than-desirable guys hanging out. They look completely bored. "Why aren't you working?" the landowner asks. Their answer? "No one hired us." So the vineyard owner makes a deal with them, and sends them off to work alongside the rest—some of whom have been hard at it since early that morning.

When it gets dark, the landowner hooks up with the fore-man of the vineyard and tells him how much to pay the vari-ous men who had worked during the day. The instructions he gives are completely bizarre—he tells the foreman to give every worker a full day's pay. *Every* worker. A hundred bucks for everybody. Doesn't matter if they started early in the morning or late in the afternoon. Doesn't matter whether they worked for eight hours or eight minutes. Everyone gets the same paycheck.

Result? The first guys on the job are ticked. They've been toil-ing in the hot sun all day, yet they get paid the same as the bozos who showed up right before the closing bell. The hard workers gripe about the unfairness, but they hardly have a point—it's not like they didn't get paid. They *did*. Everyone benefited from the ridiculously generous landowner.

End of story.

If you ask me, this story is one of the best parts of the Bible. In case you haven't figured it out yet, Jesus is the landowner. He's handing out hundred-dollar bills like bubblegum. And it doesn't matter how hard you work or how good you are at the job. You're getting the reward. All you have to do is grab it when it flies by.

That's what faith is. Faith is having the guts to grab some-thing and cling to it—and reap the rewards—even if it doesn't always make total sense. Even if it makes people mad. And what

> **THE REAL DEAL:**
>
> It doesn't matter how hard we work at being holy or how good we are at being a Christian. God loves us so much he rewards us with the gift of eternal life.

is it we're grabbing? Grace. Because God loves us so much, it doesn't matter how hard we work at being holy or how good we are at being a Christian, we're still rewarded with the gift of eternal life. We get to slosh around in God's mess of mercy.

The parable of the workers in the vineyard is what comes to mind when I think of faith, religion, and the soul. And my faith begins and ends with Jesus. I'm a Christian. Not just because I grew up in a Christian family or because I belong to a Christian church, but because I think Christianity offers something different from all the other religions in the world. And that something different is grace. And that grace comes from Jesus.

Grace is the big story of the Christian life. Ask me what makes my faith different from Islam or Buddhism or whatever else, and I'll tell you it's the freewheeling love of Jesus. It's the same paycheck going to the hard workers *and* the slackers. It's a senseless gift of God. We can't earn it. We don't deserve it. But he gives it to us anyway, for free. Crazy free.

FIRST, A LITTLE THEOLOGY

This chapter, as you probably noticed when you started reading it, is about faith. And if we're going to talk about the importance of faith—specifically, the Christian version of faith—then we need to discuss some basic points before we really get going. We need to make sure we're all on the same page.

As a Christian, I believe several things very strongly. The first is that each of us has a soul. Which basically means that, as a human, I'm not just a collection of blood and guts and bones and skin and hair. I've got something else inside me— my personality, my mind, my essence, my "innermost being"—that makes me eternal. Something that will live on after my body goes dusty. I hope the dust-turning part happens a long time from now, but when it *does* happen, I believe my soul will continue.

The second thing I believe as a Christian is that I'm a complete screwup. If you read the Bible, you'll find a lot of stuff in it about sin. What's sin? According to the Bible, it's when we rebel against God. Have you ever broken the law? Disobeyed your parents? Lied? Cheated? Focused on yourself at the expense of others? Ignored someone in need? Acted like a full-fledged jerk? Congratulations: You're a sinner. So am I. So is everyone else. All have sinned, the Bible says. All of us fall short of the glory of God. My soul—which God created—is nasty with the sin I gunked it up with. That's what happens when you're human.

The third thing I believe as a Christian is the good part. It's the part about Jesus. That, as the Son of God, he made the ultimate sacrifice and gave his life for my sin. Because God and sin couldn't coexist, Jesus died on the cross, taking the punishment for all my rebellion. All *your* rebellion, too. And because Jesus didn't stay dead, but came back to life, sin and death were defeated, and all the crap dirtying up our souls was wiped clean. Not because we earned or deserved it, but for free. Grace showed up with gallons of Soul Wash. By believing in Christ, we become new creations. Clean again. Right with God again. Saved by our faith in God, through the work of Jesus.

> **BIG TIP:**
>
> Belief is a personal choice. Faith isn't about what your parents or pastor believe. It's about what you believe. Your faith has to be your own.

FAITH IS NOT A BUNCH OF DO'S AND DON'TS

What does faith in Christ look like? Maybe not what you'd think. A lot of us get the mistaken impression that being a Christian is about following a set of rules, a list of do's and don'ts—mostly don'ts. As in, Christians don't cuss, Christians don't drink, Christians don't smoke, Christians don't go to R-rated movies.

As for the things we do, a lot of us have a checklist mentality. None of us would admit to this, but it's almost like we make a list of good Christian deeds and cross them off each day so we can feel obedient and holy. Here's what an average guy's list might look like:

> ➤ Pray.

> ➤ Read the Bible.

> ➤ Go to church.

> ➤ Listen to Christian music.

> ➤ Tell another person about Jesus.

> ➤ Resist the temptation to cuss, smoke, drink, and look at porn.

Those things are all great, but seriously—is that all the Christian life is about? Is counting the number of times a person prays each day the only way to tell he's living a faithful life? Is the true gauge of spirituality whether or not you start the morning with a little Bible reading? No. God's more interested in the big picture. Christians don't stand out from the world because of what they eat or drink or watch or don't watch. They stand out because of what and who they are. And that goes way deeper than the How-to-Be-Good lists we make.

I used to think a life of faith was about keeping the checklist, until I discovered grace. Grace means God has given us eternal life and joy and hope and peace for free. Free. Like the slackers who started working at the end of the day but got the paycheck anyway, we didn't earn it. We *can't* earn it by following the rules. We can only accept it and live grateful lives because of it.

STEP TO MANHOOD #61

Realizing that Christianity isn't about surface stuff like "being good" or following a list of rules, but about the condition of your heart.

And that's the whole story. That's the good news you keep hearing about when you go to church or read the Bible. Being a Christian is not about adhering to a certain code of holiness (and every church or youth group seems to have its own code). It's not about the law. It's about grace. God has taken care of everything. He's done everything that's required for our salvation, and there's absolutely nothing we can do to save ourselves. Nothing. Zip. Nada.

So does that mean Christians are free to run around wallowing in grace and surfing porn sites and cheating and lying and looking out for our own interests? Maybe. God might be crazy enough to still give you the hundred bucks even after you do all that stuff right to his face. But one thing that happens when you're shown such extravagant love is, you want to return it. That's where obedience comes in. Obedience is our grateful response to grace. It's how we say "Thanks" to God. It's *not* what we do to earn it.

FAITH IS A LIFESTYLE

The great thing about faith is its ability to clean up and change your soul. That's a big deal. In fact, it's such a big deal that this whole section of the book is about the soul—about who you are inside. That's what faith is about, too. It's about the condition of your heart and your outlook on life. It's about your character—how you respond to the junk the world throws at you.

But, you're still asking, *what does that inside stuff look like? How do I do it? What do I strive for?*

Honestly, there are tons of answers. One hundred people could write this chapter and come up with one hundred different ideas of what faith looks like. But I can only write what works for me, so the following characteristics of a life of faith are the ones that seem important from my very limited perspective. And since I don't personally carry a whole lot of authority, I'm backing them up with Bible verses. So there.

CONCERN FOR OTHERS

"As God's chosen people, holy and dearly loved, clothe yourselves with compassion, kindness, humility, gentleness and patience" (Colossians 3:12).

That's a long list of stuff we should "put on" each day as our spiritual clothing, but what each of those attitudes boils down to is a concern for others. *Compassion* is defined as an awareness and deep concern for another's struggles. *Kindness* is being warm-hearted in the way you interact with people. *Humility* is considering others more important than yourself. *Gentleness* is approaching others with a softness of spirit. *Patience* is allowing others the freedom to mess up, and understanding them when they do. All these things may fly in the face of society's typical definition of hard-edged manliness, but that's because, well, society is wrong. Professional wrestlers are not the manly ideal. Rappers are not the manly ideal. Stars of violent movies are not the manly ideal. Who *is*? Jesus. Concern for others is one of the manliest—or most Christlike—traits a guy could have.

WISDOM

"Be very careful, then, how you live—not as unwise but as wise, making the most of every opportunity, because the days are evil" (Ephesians 5:15–16).

On a daily basis you're faced with choices. Some of them are small: Which shirt should I wear? Whom should I invite to homecoming? Which test should I study for first? Others are big: Should I cheat on my history exam? Should I accept that beer? Should I try to go any further with my girlfriend?

How you answer those major questions says a lot about your character. Teens—especially teen guys—get a bad rap at times for making dumb decisions, for thinking with their lower heads instead of their main ones. Don't let this be you. You've got common sense. God's given you a working brain. It's up to you to put it to use. Before you make a big decision, be careful. Consider the consequences. Ask yourself questions. What might happen if I *do* accept that beer? Where might it lead if I *do* touch her there? How will I feel tomorrow? How will *she* feel?

If you're even *considering* those questions, you're way ahead of most guys. Looking beyond immediate gratification is a huge chunk of living wisely, and the first step toward making good choices.

GRATITUDE

"Give thanks to the LORD, for he is good; his love endures forever" (Psalm 107:1).

My granddad was a prisoner of war in Nazi Germany during World War II. He almost died when his plane was shot down, but he bailed out. He almost died when a crusty old German farmer found him on his property and leveled a rifle at him, but he survived. He almost died in a Nazi prison, but he escaped during a death march. All of that happened over the course of a year six decades ago. Had he died, you wouldn't be reading this book, because I wouldn't be here. Neither would my dad, who was born after my PawPaw returned home. My family as I know it wouldn't exist, either. And that's just one branch in my family tree. What if my mom had died before I came along? Or one of my great-grandfathers or great-grandmothers?

Here's the point: The chances that I exist at all are infinitesimal. Which is a big word for really stinkin' small. Technically speaking, I shouldn't be here. Any blip in my family tree and I'm nonexistent. That I'm alive at all is a gift of God. And I truly believe that.

How does that make me feel? Very thankful. Just glad to be breathing.

A lot of guys, though, look at the world differently. They act like they're owed something. They think the world revolves around them. They strut around and expect everyone to care about them, to be interested in whatever they have to say, to tell them how cool they are. Don't be that guy. It's easy to pinpoint a guy who's got a shriveled-up raisin for a soul—it's the dude who's full of himself. Because a man of faith is a man who is humble. He's a man who is glad just to be alive, and who celebrates every day as a gift. He doesn't take anything for granted, from his friends to his family to his ability to walk or run or throw a ball.

The best way to go through life is to get this straight: The world doesn't owe you anything. You owe God everything. Be grateful.

> **BIG TIP:**
>
> The best way to live life is as if just being here is the hugest gift you could have ever received. Because you know what? It is.

JOY, HOPE, OPTIMISM

"Finally, brothers, whatever is true, whatever is noble, whatever is right, whatever is pure, whatever is lovely, whatever is admirable—if anything is excellent or praiseworthy—think about such things" (Philippians 4:8).

You've heard this verse before. Most likely it was in a book or a magazine article or a sermon about keeping your mind pure, about listening to clean music or not watching certain TV shows. That's a popular interpretation of the passage, and if that's what you think it means, that's cool.

But I'm not sure that's the point Paul's trying to make. Due to the world we live in, there will be times we have to think about bad stuff, stuff that's not noble or right or pure or lovely in the least. There's even stuff like that in the Bible—a lot of sex and violence and bad attitudes and outright rebellion. (Read the book of Judges, for instance.) The fact is, you can't read the Bible without being exposed to the non-lovely. You can't live in the world today without being exposed to the non-admirable. It's all around us.

What Paul means, I think, is that our focus ought to be on the positive things. As men of faith, we ought to be optimistic.

Criticism comes naturally to most of us, but next time you feel like harshing someone, or complaining about something, or jumping ahead to the worst-case scenario—stop. See if you can twist that thought into something positive. We ought to look for the good stuff. And when we find it, we're on it like dogs on bacon.

FINAL WORDS OF WISDOM

A chapter about what faith is could go on forever. Unfortunately, this book can't. We're nearing the end of our 208 pages. So to close it up, I want to give you three more pieces of advice. Here they are:

1. It All Comes Down to Jesus

The Bible can be a confusing book. Christianity—with all its denominations and divisions and doctrines—can be a confusing religion. But there's one thing about it that's really, really simple: Jesus. He's the reason I'm a Christian. His example is behind most of the good choices I make. The only time I really feel that I'm succeeding as a believer is when I treat people the way Jesus seemed to. If you want to learn about grace, read about Jesus. If you want to find out what Christianity is all about, read about Jesus. If you want to figure out what faith looks like, read about Jesus. As unoriginal as it may be, that's the best possible advice I could give you.

> **THE REAL DEAL:**
>
> Wanna know what faith looks like? What grace is? How to treat people? Look to Jesus.

2. Find a Role Model

After you check out Jesus, find a godly man at church or in your family and model your life after his. It can be hard to apply some of the stuff in the Bible to everyday life in 2004. I understand that. For a more applicable example, look for a reliable, Christlike role model and try to follow *his* example. The best way to learn how to put faith to work is to watch another person do it, then to mimic him.

3. Never Stop Growing

I'm not the same believer I was when I first learned about Jesus as a kid. I'm not the same Christian I was when I got all fired up about God in high school. My faith isn't even the same now as when I got married. Faith isn't someplace we reach at the end of a trip. Faith *is* the trip. It's always moving. Sometimes our understanding changes. Sometimes belief comes easily, but sometimes it has to be pried out of you with a lot of yelling. Whatever the case, I'd advise you to commit to making growth a major part of your faith. Read a lot. Pray a lot. Spend time with fellow believers. Ask questions. Look for answers. Why? Because, as kids, most of us accepted our parents' faith. But at some point, it has to become *our* faith in order for it to stay strong. The best way for that to happen is for you to put it through a regular workout. And don't worry—God can handle it.

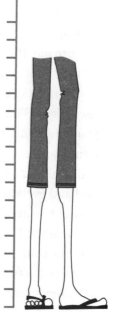

CHAPTER 14

YOUR NEIGHBOR

Back in the first century, when Jesus began his public ministry, all the religious people lived under a bunch of rules. Hundreds of them. There were rules about what to wear and how to eat and what constituted "work" on the Sabbath day. The religious people thought they were being super holy because they followed all the tiny little details of the law. Then Jesus came around and started breaking some of those rules, and all the religious people—they were called Pharisees—got annoyed.

People were always asking Jesus a lot of questions. Makes sense to me. If I were standing on a hillside with the Son of God, I'd have a lot of questions, too. (One of them would be "Why in the world did you create mosquitoes?") At one point, some lawyer-type Pharisee asked Jesus to identify the greatest commandment in the law. He was trying to trick Jesus into proclaiming one more important than the rest, which would have gotten him in trouble again with the holy joes. But Jesus—being God and everything—figured out their game, and gave them an answer they weren't expecting.

"Love the Lord your God," he said, "with all your heart and with all your soul and with all your mind" (Matthew 22:37). That was the first and greatest commandment, Jesus told them, but there's another one that's a whole lot like it: *Love your neighbor as yourself.* He explained that all the commandments of God hinge on those two statements.

Love God. Love your neighbor.

That's one of the reasons I like Jesus so much. He took hundreds of complicated rules and condensed them into just two simple ones. And he did it in a way that annoyed the religious people. I probably shouldn't say this, but I kind of like that, too.

Here in America today, we Christians put a lot of effort into fulfilling the first part of what Jesus told us to do. We focus a lot on loving the Lord with all our hearts, souls, minds, and strength. We get really into stuff like singing worship songs at church, which makes us feel close to God. We listen to Christian music and go to Christian concerts and attend Christian festivals. We read Christian books (like this one!) and go to Christian camps or youth conferences or discipleship events. We talk a lot about sexual purity (which is good) and spending time with God (which is good) and reading the Bible (which is also good). We also spend a lot of time worrying about the morality of societal issues like abortion and gay marriage and the decline of values. We do all this stuff because we believe God wants us to and because we think it's a way for us to show him we love him with all our hearts, souls, minds, and strength. And that's fine. Good for us.

But I get the feeling that we're so focused on personal holiness and a lifestyle of worship and moral purity and having purpose-driven lives that we forget about part two of the Great Commandment—the part about loving our neighbors. We don't realize that loving people is one of the most important ways we can show love to God. Singing worship songs and going to church are great, but if you're only doing that without showing love to everyone you come into contact with, then you're only doing half of what Jesus told us we should be doing.

THE REAL DEAL:

If you're only focusing on your relationship with God without showing love to other people, then you're only doing half of what Jesus said we should be doing.

A lot of us are half-Christian. Adults, teens, preachers, regular church people, whomever. We're experts (in our minds) at the loving-God part. But occasionally we lose sight of the love-your-neighbor part.

Yep. I'm saying "we" and "our" and "us." I'm a half-Christian, too.

WHO IS MY NEIGHBOR?

A better question would be: Who is *not* my neighbor? Because when Jesus said to love your neighbor, I didn't catch any *except*s or *unless*es or *but*s tacked onto the end of the commandment. For instance, he didn't say the following:

> ➤ Love your neighbor as yourself, unless your neighbor is a mega dweeb.

> ➤ Love your neighbor as yourself, except for gay people.

> ➤ Love your neighbor as yourself, unless he's a Democrat.

> ➤ Love your neighbor as yourself, but don't give money to homeless people because they'll spend it on booze.

> ➤ Love your neighbor as yourself, except for atheists.

> ➤ Love your neighbor as yourself, unless she believes in evolution.

Or even this:

> ➤   Love your neighbor as yourself, so you can get him to come to church and become a Christian.

The thing is, we're pretty good at loving people who are just like us. Our churches are full of the same kinds of people, and anyone who doesn't quite fit into that mold isn't always guaranteed a welcome mat or a friendly smile when they come in the door. We want our neighbors to look and act and think just like we do.

That's the way the religious people back in Jesus' society used to think. They were all for loving their neighbor, as long as that neighbor was of their own race and religion. Sinners, though? Not their neighbors. Tax collectors like Zacchaeus? Not their neighbors. Samaritans, Gentiles, lepers? Nope, nope, and nope. Those people got no love.

STEP TO MANHOOD #20

Showing love to people just because, with no strings attached

Then Jesus came along, and he hung out with drunkards and prostitutes and other professional sinners. He spent time with tax collectors, who were hated by the culture. He kicked it with people who were considered unclean, like lepers. He buddied with the people he wasn't supposed to be friends with. Jesus showed the world that everyone is our neighbor—no strings attached—and that no one should be denied the love of God. Even if they don't end up coming to church with you. Even if they're not interested in becoming a Christian. That stuff is for God to worry about. Your job is to show love to people.

HOW DO I DO IT?

Glad you asked. There are lots of ways to show God's love. Some of those ways are interior, "nonaction" behaviors. You can pray for people. You can keep an open mind. You can change your attitude toward the "outcasts." Back in the New Testament, outcasts were tax collectors and lepers and Samaritans. Today they may be homeless people or homosexuals or people who otherwise have been shunned by society. We're so used to ignoring people who aren't like us that it takes a major mental turnaround to look at them like Jesus looks at them—as someone he loves enough to die for, even if they aren't interested in loving him back. That's something we need to realize, but it can be hard.

But the best way to show God's love to people is through action. Love is best expressed by doing stuff. Remember the story of the Good Samaritan? Jesus used it to teach his listeners about being a good neighbor. When a guy was beaten up and robbed and left for dead along the road, two people passed him by before a despised Samaritan (a member of a race of people who were societal outcasts) stopped to help him. The first guy that passed by was a priest. He probably said a prayer for the guy, but kept walking. The second was another churchy guy, a Levite. He might have had a compassionate thought or two upon seeing the dude in a bloody heap, but he didn't spring into action.

The Samaritan, though? He *showed* love. He didn't just feel it. He cleaned the guy up, took him back into town, paid for a room he could rest in, and generally took care of the guy until he recovered. That's love. The best way to show love is by doing stuff. Giving back to your church or society. Sharing from the blessings God has given you. Doing charity work. Volunteering.

BIG TIP:

The best way to show God's love to people is through action. Love is best expressed by doing stuff.

WHAT CAN I DO?

Again, glad you asked. The one thing I want to do in this chapter is to give you some ideas of how you can give back to society, how you can make the concept of loving your neighbor into something concrete and real, rather than just a happy little idea. Let's start on a small-scale, interpersonal basis and move up from there.

SMALL-SCALE

Be kind every chance you get. This one's fairly easy: Be nice. The world needs a lot more nice. It's easy to get grouchy and sullen and to perfect the art of the teenage pout, but it takes a real man to be different from every other kid in the world. It takes a real man to actually practice kindness. What does kindness look like? It looks like a smile. It means being friendly. It means greeting people when you pass them at school or on the street. It means treating people with respect. It means refusing to bully or tease at school. Not only does it mean not participating when some kid is being picked on, it means standing up for that kid. Being friendly may be popular, but protecting the underdog? Not so much. Not necessarily that cool. Then again, Jesus didn't say much about being cool. **Cost:** *Nothing.*

Refuse to ignore the homeless guy on the corner.

I once knew an old, frail Episcopal priest who pastored several rural churches. He used to drive a lot during the week, and he would always pick up hitchhikers. This guy was ancient. He weighed about 120 pounds. If one really wanted to, some hitcher could toss him out the door and steal his Lincoln without even breaking a sweat. That's why everyone who knew the priest always asked him to quit picking up every thumb bum he saw. "I can't," the priest always said. "One of them might be Jesus."

In Matthew 25, Jesus says that whenever you do something for the "least of these"—the sick, the poor, the needy—then you're actually doing it for him. That means making eye contact with the old hairy homeless dude with the "Please Help" sign. Why? Because you're really looking into Jesus' eyes. Once you've acknowledged a homeless guy and treated him like a real person, try to help in some small way. Give him a dollar. Give him the change from your ashtray. Give him the benefit of the doubt. Sure, he may go out and spend your buck on cheap wine and cigarettes, but why not trust him to use it wisely? If that still seems too risky for you, then keep some coupons or gift certificates in your car, and hand those out. Some people keep a "car kit" in the backseat. It's not filled with food, but with toiletries like soap, wet wipes, a toothbrush, deodorant, and maybe even the locations and phone numbers of local homeless shelters. If you don't want to give them money, at least give them something useful.

But don't give them the cold shoulder. That is, unless you're comfortable ignoring Jesus. **Cost:** *Depends on what you give.*

Get rid of your old stuff.

If you're like me, you have too many pairs of jeans, too many pairs of shoes, too many shirts. You have socks you don't wear, and last season's cords, and clothes you outgrew two years ago. Your closet is full, but you're still growing, so every year you're piling up old stuff that doesn't fit. Resist the urge to sell it on consignment or in a garage sale. Instead, give it to charity, to someone who'll treasure it (check with your parents first, though, before you give away something they paid for). The Salvation Army is always in need of decent clothing. Homeless shelters, too. In fact, most homeless people would give anything for new clothing. Instead of a handful of change, why not give your old shoes or jacket to the guy on the street corner? **Cost:** *Old stuff you don't wear anymore.*

MEDIUM-SCALE

Visit a nursing home or retirement center.

When I was a senior in high school, I used to deliver prescription drugs for a pharmacy, and lots of those deliveries went to nursing homes. I hated it. The hallways were always lined with sad, near-dead men and women in wheelchairs, and it was all I could do to get out of there as fast as I could. Now, I regret the attitude I used to have. I regret it a lot. Because how would I feel if I had to spend the last years of my life in that cold, clinical environment, with no one to talk to or smile with or even look at? Honestly, I can't think of anything worse.

Thankfully, nursing homes and retirement centers have gotten much better in recent years. Many of them are lively, healthy places for senior adults. But even so, there are lots of lonely residents who are aching for someone to smile at them, to play a round of checkers with them, to sing a song or to just sit and talk. Do you play the guitar? Ask if you can bring it to the facility as a way to hone your playing-in-front-of-people skills (most of them won't be able to hear you screw up anyway). Learn some old hymns and you're golden. Or are your skills more the sitting-and-listening type? Then you're perfect. Sit down for 15 minutes and ask questions. Listen to their stories. Retirement communities and extended-care facilities are ripe with easy, inexpensive volunteer opportunities. *Cost: Your time.*

Do freebie yard work for an elderly person.

If there's one thing teenage guys are good at, it's mowing lawns. Where I live, that's what guys do during the summer. Which is fine. It's great to make money. But while you're at it, I'd challenge you to throw in a couple of yards for free. Maybe it's the widow who lives next to you and your parents, or an older couple across from one of your regular customers. Just start mowing one day. They'll probably come out and try to stuff a twenty in your hand, but you're gonna refuse to take it. You'll just say, "No thanks, this one's on me." Smile and finish the yard. If they offer you a cold drink, *always* accept. Stay and talk to them afterward—even if it's just for a few minutes—because there's nothing they like better than company, and there's no better company than the nice young man who just started mowing their yard one day for free. Thank them for the drink, then come back next week and do the whole thing again. Do it all summer and you'll have made their year. This idea is huge—I dare you to do something this selfless and impressive. *Cost: Your time and a nonprofitable yard.*

STEP TO MANHOOD #39

Working hard for free, in order to make someone's day.

Volunteer at your church.

Most kids who have grown up attending church are indebted to it. You've benefited from a place to worship, from teachers who put hours of work into helping you mature, from youth workers and ministers who invested time and effort into your life. You've taken a lot from the church. Now that you're nearly an adult, it's time to give something back. And I'm not just talking about 10 percent of your yard-mowing money (though that would be great). I'm talking about your time. For instance, churches always need workers for children and babies, whether it's helping teach a Sunday school class or simply providing a hand in the nursery. Yes—the nursery. My four-year-old daughter's favorite Sunday school "teacher" up to this point has been a seventeen-year-old kid named Erik. Erik's mother was actually my daughter's teacher, but he used to drop in every Sunday at the end of the hour. Did I mention that Erik was about six-four and 250 pounds? He'd step over the gate and the kids would pile on. The boys loved him. The girls giggled. Ellie always came home from church talking about "Mr. Erik"—and he was just a big dude who stopped by to wait for his mom. Never underestimate the adoration little kids have of guys your age. It's real. And it's fun.

Helping out with preschoolers or babies is just one of the ways you can give back to your church. There are plenty of others, from picking up trash around the grounds on Saturdays to helping administer Communion on Sundays. If you're into graphic design, maybe you could help put the bulletin together each week, or keep the church Web site updated. Ask any one of the ministers if there's something you can do. I guarantee they'll say yes. **Cost:** *Your time.*

Work on a Habitat for Humanity house.

Since 1976, Habitat for Humanity has built more than one hundred thousand homes all over the world for families without decent housing. The homes are built by the homeowners themselves—who have to pay for the home via a special interest-free mortgage—along with teams of volunteers (plus an expert or two to keep things in line). People of all ages and skill levels are welcome to help out. If you know a thing or two about carpentry or plumbing or electrical work, then you're ideally suited for this kind of community service. If the phrase *two-by-four* sounds like a math problem to you, then Habitat's an ideal place for you to learn a thing or two about construction. Have fun, gain some real-world skills, and help out a deserving family—who could ask for a better way to give back? **Cost:** *Your time.*

LARGE-SCALE

Participate in a short-term mission trip.

Maybe a team from your church is going to Germany to run a sports clinic. Maybe they're traveling to Mexico to help restore an orphanage, or to Guatemala for a church construction project. Short-term missions are a way for laypeople (church members who are not paid ministers) to participate in missions. They are usually one- or two-week trips, often to foreign countries, and revolve around some sort of service project. Sometimes the

> **BIG TIP:**
>
> Short-term missions aren't sightseeing trips or exotic vacations. They're work. Lazies need not apply.

goal is simply to show love to people by providing the time, energy, and resources to help meet a need. At other times, the willingness to work on a project is viewed as a way to build relationships with people of other cultures in order to tell them about Jesus. Short-term missions, however, are not to be taken lightly. They aren't sightseeing trips or exotic vacations. They're work. Fulfilling work, but work all the same. Not for lazy people. *Cost: Depends on where you're going, but usually expensive due to airfare, lodging, etc.*

Sponsor a child.

Through ministries like Compassion International or WorldVision, you can sponsor a child who lives in poverty somewhere in the world. When you sponsor a child, you get linked with one particular child who will know your name and write letters to you. Even better, they'll know there is someone in the world who loves them and wants to help them. Here's how it works: For a monthly fee, sponsored children get connected with church-based programs that provide them with educational opportunities, better nutrition, good health care, and spiritual development. This is the kind of thing that can literally change a kid's life. My family is currently sponsoring a little girl named Maria, who lives in Columbia. She sends us letters and fun, glittery pictures every couple of months. ***Cost: $28 a month to sponsor a child through Compassion (www.compassion.com); $26 a month to sponsor a child through WorldVision (www.worldvision.org). If that amount is too much for you on a monthly basis, you might consider splitting the cost among several people. Could each member of your Sunday school class pitch in a few dollars every month to sponsor a child? What about your soccer team or youth group?***

Give a meaningful gift to the poor.

Sponsoring a child isn't the only way to help the poor. Ministries like WorldVision or Samaritan's Purse have extensive donation plans in place that allow you to make one-time gifts to meet unique needs. For instance, through WorldVision, you could give a gift of $15 to provide a needy child with brand-new clothing, replacing the nasty rags he or she has to wear. In some drought-stricken parts of Africa, schools are closing because the children are too weak and hungry to learn. For just $16—the cost of, for instance, two or three trips to Burger King—you can pay to provide seeds, farming tools, and training to a drought-affected family, giving them everything they need to grow several months' worth of food. (Check out www.worldvision.org for dozens more creative ways to help the world's poor.)

Another relief organization, Samaritan's Purse, offers a bunch of interesting gift ideas to help the sick and suffering people of the world. For $50 you can give a dairy goat to a family in Honduras. The goat produces several quarts of milk every day, which the family can drink straight or use to make cheese and butter. Or, you can give $9 to their infant-feeding project, which is enough to feed a malnourished baby for a week (there is nothing more heartbreaking to me than the thought of a helpless baby crying because she's hungry). You can also give the gift of chicks: $10 can provide a brood of twenty-four baby chickens that can grow into a flock of egg-laying hens for a family. The family can then use the eggs for food, and sell the rest at market. (Visit www.samaritanspurse.org for many more practical, unique ways to give.) **Cost: Depends on what you give, but almost any amount can be put to use in a practical way.**

Help raise awareness for AIDS in Africa.

More than 9,500 Africans are infected with HIV/AIDS every day. More than 6,500 die from it daily, 1,400 of whom are children who got the disease from drinking their mothers' breast milk. One in two Africans are under twenty—your age—but chances are good they won't live to see twenty-five. Why? Because the AIDS virus has been ravaging the continent for years, and the numbers are only getting worse. Experts suggest there will be twenty million AIDS orphans (children who have lost one or both parents to AIDS) by the year 2010. Entire generations are dying out. To fight the problem, organizations like DATA (Debt, AIDS, Trade Africa—www.data.org) are working to help raise government resources, to provide much-needed treatment, medication, and education to the African people on the issue. Also, go to www.theonecampaign.org to learn more about how you can fight global AIDS and poverty.

What can you do to fight AIDS in Africa? Plenty. You can support legislation by writing or e-mailing your congressional representative about the African AIDS crisis, asking him or her to support legislation on the issue (to congressional representatives, one handwritten

> **THE REAL DEAL:**
>
> The African AIDS epidemic has become the major health issue of our time, and it's not going away anytime soon.

letter is equivalent to one hundred of their constituents). You can help raise awareness by telling your friends about the crisis. You can write letters to the editor of your local newspaper. You can hook up your youth leaders or pastor with resources to help them learn and teach about the issue. You can suggest mission trips to Africa to work in AIDS orphanages or minister to hurting families. You can help plan those trips. And you can pray.

Cost: *Millions of dollars to provide education and health care to Africa, most of which will be given by governments or philanthropy organizations. The major thing you can give is your time, passion, and interest.*

ONE FINAL THOUGHT

If you live in the United States, then you've pretty much got it made. Compared to the rest of the world, you're privileged. If you can afford to buy this book, you're wealthier than most people on earth. You may not be dripping with bling or rollin' in Bentleys, but as an American, you live in luxury. Your biggest problem may be a zit breakout the day before homecoming. Some teens' problems include having no place to live, no decent clothing, and no parents, thanks to AIDS. Hard to comprehend, but true.

There's a passage in Luke 12 where Jesus tells a crowd of people something that can be summarized this way: *To whom much is given, much is required.* In Philippians, Paul explains it in a little more detail. "Each of you should look not only to your own interests," he writes, "but also to the interests of others. Your attitude should be the same as that of Christ Jesus" (2:4–5). In other words, be like Jesus, and don't get so caught up in yourself that you forget about others.

Which leads us back to what we discussed at the very beginning of this chapter. Best way to love God? By loving others. Get off your butt and give it a go.

For more volunteering ideas or opportunities, visit the International Association for Volunteer Effort (www.iave.org) or Action Without Borders (www.idealist.org).

CHAPTER 15

WHAT'S NEXT?

So here we are. Last chapter. Just a few pages to go, and if this book's subtitle is to be believed, you're just a few pages away from manhood. Good job with that. Thanks for tuning in.

But is it really that easy? Nope. Physically, it's no worry. You pretty much become a man on your own once the hormones kick in. No trouble at all, if you can handle a year or two of complete and total awkwardness. The body takes care of it. But mentally? That's another story. Manhood of the mind isn't something that happens on autopilot. Instead, it's a process of maturing, of learning to think and make wise choices. Easier said than done.

And spiritually? Spiritual manhood is also a process. I know a few eighteen-year-olds who, when it comes to the soul, are all-out men. They're impressive. I also know some thirty-year-olds who, sadly, are *not* men. They're spiritual babies. They're running around with souls in diapers.

Part of growing up happens naturally. Part of it happens because of the choices you make. Hopefully this book has touched on both sides of that road to manhood, and hopefully you're a little farther down it as a result.

Here's the deal. You could read a book like this every day of the week and still never feel properly equipped for the stuff that comes along. As a teenager, you're dealing with all kinds of unique stress. Keeping your grades up. Trying to make the team. Fitting in with your friends. Remembering to check your fly each morning.

And once you graduate from high school—which may be a few years away or very soon, depending on your age—you're gonna face a whole new set of pressures. College. Scholarships. Serious dating. Full-time jobs.

There will be times when it all seems to work out perfectly, and you'll be on top of the world. And there will be times when you feel like you're battling whales with a bag of weenies and a Snoopy pole.

Let me be the first to tell you that's okay. Feeling inadequate is expected at this age. It's normal to feel like you don't have all the resources—physical, mental, spiritual—you need to make it through each day. That's why God gave us things like prayer. Like the strength of Christian friends. Like the wisdom of the Bible. Like (gulp) our parents.

But that doesn't mean there's nothing you can do to prepare for the challenges of life—especially the ones that are still a few years away. In fact, recent surveys have indicated that three out of four high-school students—guys and girls—devote a great amount of thought to life after high school. Hopefully you're one of them. The best way to take hold of your future is to look ahead, to get some idea of what's coming and to start to plan accordingly. That's the purpose of this chapter. It's the end of the book but the beginning of a whole lot more.

Specifically, we're gonna cover

> **BIG TIP:**
>
> Three out of four high-school students devote a great amount of thought to life after high school. Make sure you do, too.

stuff that will soon become major to you once you leave the high-school scene and blast into college. It's about direction—where you'll go and who you'll become as an adult. Put on your seat belt.

EDUCATION

WHAT ABOUT IT?

Once you've graduated from high school, most of your friends will probably begin attending a college or university. Regardless of how old you are, the best time to start preparing for that big move is now.

WHAT ARE MY OPTIONS?

There are plenty. You can shoot for the stars and try to get into an Ivy League university (Harvard, Princeton) or one of the top private schools like Stanford, Rice, or Duke. These will cost a lot but offer a premier education. Nothing looks better on your résumé than a degree from one of these schools.

Another option is to attend a public, state-sponsored university (UCLA, the University of Texas, Ohio State University). You'll still get a great education, but the cost will be significantly lower. State schools are almost always a lot larger than private schools, so expect bigger class sizes.

Or, you can start out at a two-year junior college that's close to home, then transfer to a larger school later. This is the least expensive option, but still a good one.

HOW DO I PAY FOR IT?

The cost of going to college can be enormously expensive. Thankfully, there are plenty of options to help pay for it. First, there's the free money. Every college or university offers scholarships. These can be merit-based (awarding you for academic talent or a certain skill, like musical ability or athletics) or need-based (which takes your financial situation

> **THE REAL DEAL:**
>
> Going to college will cost major bucks. Thankfully, there are plenty of options to help pay for it.

into account). Other free money comes in the form of government grants like the Pell Grant. Scholarships and grants usually require you to keep a certain grade point average or class load, but you don't have to pay them back.

Other options include federal or private student loans (which you do have to pay back), work-study programs (which provide you a job to help offset college costs), or military service (which lets you earn money for college by signing up for full-time or part-time military duty). And most states and financial institutions now offer great college savings plans for parents. If high-school graduation is still a few years away, you might ask your parents if they've set up a college savings plan in your name. It's never too late.

WHAT SHOULD I BE DOING NOW?

Depends on your age. If you're a high-school junior or senior, you need to begin thinking seriously about college and going through the application process. If you're younger than that, just keep the above options in the back of your mind. Keep your grades up, so you remain attractive to admissions and scholarship boards. Participate in the kinds of extracurricular activities (community service, student government, etc.) that will look good on your applications. And if you can, start saving money now. Ask your parents if you can contribute some of your yard-mowing money to your college savings plan. They'll think you're the best son ever, and every little bit helps.

WORK

WHAT ABOUT IT?

What do you want to be when you grow up? That's not just a question for college guys to ask themselves. In a recent poll, 84 percent of teens said they had given a fair amount of consideration to eventual career or job plans. More than half of those surveyed said they had given the topic very serious thought. Should it be something you stress about between high-school chemistry projects? No way. But it is something you might be applying your brain to during its off-hours.

WHAT ARE MY OPTIONS?

A better way to put it is what aren't your options? Because at this stage in life, you can pretty much do or be whatever you want. It's your life, your dream, your career. Unless you're five-foot-three and want to be an NBA star, the possibilities are limitless. Current hot careers include those in the healthcare industry, such as pharmacists, biochemists, occupational therapists, and paramedics. Education is another always-growing career field, especially if you're bilingual. Good with computers? Information systems managers, data communications analysts, and software engineers are major growth occupations. In fact, anything tech-related will still be in demand a few years from now. Combine tech with health and you're golden.

WHAT SHOULD I BE DOING NOW?

Looking around. Observing. Asking questions. Getting some foot-in-the-door experience. Want specifics? First, get involved at school. Join school clubs or organizations that do stuff related to what you're interested in. Thinking about a career in medicine? Check out the science or biology club. A budding

> **BIG TIP:**
> Don't get all weird about it, but don't let these opportunities go to waste either.

entrepreneur? Consider student organizations like DECA (an association for students interested in marketing, management, and entrepreneurship) or SIFE (Students in Free Enterprise). Second, participate in career day if your school sponsors one. Third, ask your school counselors if they know of any summer jobs or internships related to whatever careers you're interested in. Above all, ask your parents or teachers about certain career options. Chances are, they know someone in those professions and can tell you about them. Don't get all frantic and weird about it, but don't let these opportunities go to waste, either. Your teen years are a great time to start thinking about the rest of your life.

MONEY

WHAT ABOUT IT?

At some point in life, you're gonna need it. *Duh.* And what you do with it then—how you handle it from day to day, week to week—is often determined by habits you learn as a teen.

And learning good financial habits now should be a priority. Why? Because more young people than ever are digging financial holes for themselves before they're even out of college. Around 150,000 adults between the ages of eighteen and twenty-five declare bankruptcy each year. And bankruptcy is bad. Once it hits your financial record, it's stuck like a spaghetti stain.

WHAT ARE MY OPTIONS?

There are two. Option one: You learn to handle a small amount of money now, as a smart teenager. You learn about saving. About spending less then you earn. About the dangers of credit cards. About the value of making good, planned purchases. About setting a budget and sticking to it. Then, once the adult money starts rolling in, you use it wisely and live a life free of financial problems. Or option two: You spend whatever's in your wallet. You make brainless financial decisions. You treat money carelessly, then you go into mega-debt by the time you're twenty-five. You can't buy a car. You can't buy a house. You have trouble renting an apartment. You have collection agencies calling all hours of the day. You can't keep a girlfriend because you're always mooching off her. Your life is ruined because you never learned how to use money. So . . . which will it be? Option one or two?

WHAT SHOULD I BE DOING NOW?

If you're younger than sixteen, it may be hard to get a "real" job, so to earn money you may have to do chores for your parents or grandparents. Maybe you mow some yards. Help paint the house. Do what you can to earn a little money. If you're older than sixteen, find an afterschool or weekend or summer job. Work hard.

Once you've got the money, tell yourself this: *I can't have everything I want whenever I want it.* Say it until you start to annoy yourself, because this is something you'll need to remember your whole life. Most people can't buy whatever they want whenever they want it. But some do anyway, and this is where the trouble starts.

STEP TO MANHOOD #45

Realizing you can't buy whatever you want whenever you want it.

If there's something you want to buy—a car, a stereo, a computer—save for it first. Get your parents to help you set a budget. Stash away part of every paycheck. If you want something, it's better to save for it than to look for the instant gratification of buying it on credit (such as with a credit card). Credit cards can get you into trouble. Whenever you can, save and buy stuff with cash. Keep up with what you do spend. Shop around to get the best deal. Above all, stay in control of your money and enjoy the freedom that control gives you. Because once you lose control, you'll be miserable. Just ask half the people in the United States who are neck-deep in debt.

Finally, give part of what you have to God. Maybe to your local church. Maybe to a charity doing the work of Jesus. Maybe to someone who needs it. Why? Because it's not your money in the first place. It's his. You're just keeping it in your pocket for a little while. Give some back every chance you get.

RELATIONSHIPS

WHAT ABOUT IT?

At some point, one of those dating relationships we talked about earlier is gonna get serious. Way serious. Maybe it'll be during your college years, or after you graduate. Heck, it may be during your senior year of high school. Whenever it happens, you'll probably fall in love and start thinking about marriage. And once that starts, your life will never be the same. In a good way.

WHAT ARE MY OPTIONS?

Weird question, but here goes. Your options are exactly what you might think. You can date around and never commit, living life as a bachelor. For some people, this is a fun and carefree existence. It leaves you plenty of room for friendships with the opposite sex. And to be honest, it's great for people diligently pursuing a career or the ministry—you've got time to focus and work hard. But for others, it can be incredibly lonely. Some people are happy only when they have someone to share life with. That means marriage, and that's cool, too. Marriage is great (personally, I'm all for it), but it isn't for everyone.

WHAT SHOULD I BE DOING NOW?

Um . . . nothing. You're a teenager, remember? Unless you're living in some sort of biblical time warp, marital bliss shouldn't really be on your agenda. Don't sweat it. There can be a lot of pressure to have a girlfriend in high school, but there's no rule that says you've got to be attached to be cool. No way. Being a single teen is fine. In fact, it's preferable for a lot of guys. Doesn't mean anything's wrong. Don't stress about relationships. The right girl will come along.

What you can do as a teenager is begin to look at girls—no, not that way—in terms of what you might look for in a wife. As you build friendships with members of the opposite sex, study them. File away mental notes for the future: What physical traits attract you? Better yet, what personality traits attract you? Which character qualities

> **BIG TIP:**
>
> Don't stress about relationships during your teen years. The right girl will eventually come along.

mesh best with who you are? What kinds of things really annoy you? What kinds of interests do you want your future mate to have? Does she need to have certain religious beliefs?

Why think about this stuff now? Because whom you marry is just about the biggest decision you'll ever make. And once you reach a certain age, there's a lot of pressure—from friends, from parents, from society as a whole—to jump into the question-popping stage of life. When the pressure hits, you need to know who to listen to. First on the list is God. Look for his wisdom above all. But second is yourself. If you've spent the last several years thinking about what kind of girl you want to marry, then you'll know her when you see her. She'll be the last piece of the puzzle. It'll be an easy decision to make—and it's your decision to make, not anyone else's. That's why it doesn't hurt to get a head start.

Guys, there are a lot of choices coming up: *What will I do with my life? Where will I go to college? Whom will I marry? Who will I be?* Do you have to make all these decisions right now? No. Thank God in heaven, no. Life is stressful enough as it is.

But the answers to those questions start to spin around inside you during your formative teen years. As you grow physically and mentally. As you mature and develop your personality and niche in life. Thinking about the future is one way to start filling in some of the blanks. It's a way to be smart, to plan ahead and prepare for the challenges to come.

And those challenges are just around the corner. You're ready for them, though. All this time, just by living your life and using your brain (and reading high-quality books like this one), you've been preparing for it. All this time you've been taking small steps toward the rest of your life. It's exciting. It's a little scary. But guess what? Take care of the mind, body, and soul, and you're gonna be fine. Have fun.

CONCLUSION

Well, here we are. Last few pages of the book. So how's it going? Feeling less confused than you were? Ready for some recap questions?

A few questions: Having read this book, do you now understand what it means to be a man in our society? Are you up-to-date with all the details of etiquette and the "gentleman's code"? Are you cool with peer pressure? Can you communicate with your parents? With girls?

More questions: Are you buff, ripped, and otherwise well-exercised? Able to tie a tie? Shave a face? (Preferably your own.) Utterly at ease with your own sexuality and all the changes of puberty? Have you solved the mystery of the female gender?

Still more: Do you understand and appreciate your family? Your friends? Are you steadfast in your faith? Committed to community? Ready to face the future with grit and intelligence and all-around pizzazz?

Tired of all the questions yet? Me, too.

But here's one more: How many of those questions can you answer "Yes" to with any degree of confidence? Be honest.

My guess is that, even now, very few of us have everything figured out. Why? Because the answers to life's challenges can't be gained from reading a book, especially a little 208-page paperback that claims to turn you into a man. I'm the author of the book in question, and you know what? The only questions I can give a definitive "yes" to from the list above are the ones about shaving and tie-tying. Whoop-de-doo. I haven't automatically achieved wisdom. My self-esteem hasn't shot to the roof. I'm not bursting with certainty or understanding. Those are lifetime quests, and they don't happen overnight.

So was reading *A Guy's Guide to Life* a big, fat waste of your time? Was writing it a waste of *my* time? Not a chance. Because, hopefully, having finished the book, you know a lot more than when you started. In the process of studying and thinking about and writing about this stuff, I've certainly learned a thing or two. Chapter by chapter, I've tried to pass along info intended to fuel your mind, body, and spirit. And by the grace of God, you've gained something from it. Maybe it's insight about stuff you've never really considered before. Or answers to questions you were afraid to ask—or didn't think to ask in the first place. Advice about handling some sticky situations. A little humor and entertainment. Fun stories. Some nice graphics and a catchy layout. If so, that's good.

But more than anything else, what I want you to take away from this book is the understanding that your Mind/Body/Soul package is important to a well-lived life. That package needs to be acknowledged and cared for. Each part is important. Each part works together to support the other. Each part is vital in the process of becoming who God wants you to be.

Take care of your mind. It's your CPU, the core of your decision-making process. It allows you to understand the world we live in. It helps you communicate, build relationships, and become a contributing member of your family, your church, your school, and your society. Taking care of your mind means using it. It means asking questions and chasing after truth. It means refusing to settle for sloppy thinking or a steady diet of mental junk food like video games. It means pursuing an active, razor-sharp mind and the success that comes along with it.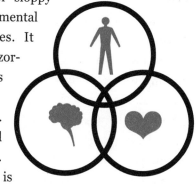

Take care of your body. Because, well, without the bod you're not getting much done. In many respects, your body is gonna take care of itself. It'll grow on its own. It'll race through puberty whether you're ready for it or not. But it also needs to be monitored. Keep it well-fed and properly rested. Don't get lazy. Don't eat trash. Exercise. And stay in control of things like your sex drive. Libido is natural, but it's not the boss. You are.

And, finally, take care of your soul. "Above all else, guard your heart," Proverbs 4:23 says, "for it is the wellspring of life." Life begins and ends with the soul. It's the inner spark that puts our bodies in motion. It's the deep stirring that whirls our minds into shape. It's the point of contact for our relationship with God, and because of that connection, everything else revolves around it. Mind. Body. Strength. Relationships. The future. All of these are centered around your "wellspring." Like a well in the desert, your soul feeds you. It nourishes you. It keeps every other aspect of life functioning. Pay attention to it, protect it, and the rest of the pieces will eventually snap into place.

Guys, thanks. It's been fun, but things are only just now getting started. So . . . welcome. Welcome to the good stuff. Welcome to the hard stuff.

Welcome to manhood.